CW00590011

Grant Hill was born in Dundee in 1979 and has predominantly worked in journalism and public relations. He worships at the altar of Keith Wright and Tommy Coyne and is the author of the novel *Clubbed To Death*.

AK 86

TWO SHOTS IN THE HEART
OF SCOTTISH FOOTBALL

GRANT HILL

AK 86: TWO SHOTS IN THE HEART OF SCOTTISH FOOTBALL

Copyright © 2016 Grant Hill

Front cover images courtesy and copyright of **Dave Martin**

Back cover image copyright **SNS / Alamy Stock Photo**

Designed and set by **Chris Collins**

Printed in Great Britain by Bell and Bain Ltd, Glasgow.

For Mum and Dad

Saturday, 26th April 1986

It was the day that Chernobyl, a hitherto little-known Ukrainian city, became a byword for atomic folly as a catastrophic explosion that would ultimately claim tens of thousands of lives, devastate the environment and help hasten the end of the Soviet Union, ripped through the nearby nuclear power plant.

Two-and-a-half thousand miles away, the minds of the supporters and players of Heart of Midlothian Football Club were not focused on a nuclear winter but rather a glorious spring. For them, the beautiful game was truly stunning at that moment in time, an exhilarating distraction from the realities of Britain's most turbulent post-war decade.

It was an era of contradiction. Plenty and penury. Boom and bust. Excess and Orgreave. Wine bars and race riots. Shoulder pads and flying pickets. Popular culture remembers the decade style forgot, while those from the UK's industrial heartlands remember the communities their politicians abandoned.

It had taken the jingoism born in Port Stanley and the ineptitude of a bitterly divided opposition to save Margaret Thatcher from electoral disaster in the summer of 1983 but three years hence her monetarist revolution was in full swing. With victory secured over the enemy without at Goose Green and the enemy within on the coalfields that had powered the industrial revolution, the Conservative government was by now picking off what they saw as impediments to Britain's global competitiveness one by one.

The post-war consensus was torn up as the commitment to full employment was jettisoned, council houses flogged and public utilities were auctioned off to the whims of the free market. Thatcher's capitalist democracy awash with property and share ownership may have been irresistible to many but also represented the end of the certainties that generations of British families had enjoyed.

With the Poll Tax riots that would ultimately lead to her downfall still four years away, it was the high watermark of Thatcherism. Depending on which side of a polarised country you stood this was either a cause for mourning or great celebration.

At 4.40pm on Saturday, 26th April 1986, politics, economics and class war mattered little to the maroon half of Edinburgh as Tynecastle Park was rocked to its foundations by the euphoria that greeted that day's final whistle. A nervy 1-0 home win over Clydebank had moved Hearts to within a point of their first Scottish League championship since 1960. With a Scottish Cup final against Aberdeen to follow in a fortnight's time the club was now 180 minutes away from an unprecedented double. It was in a spirit of suspended celebration that 20,000 delirious Jambos spilled out from the terraces into the streets of Gorgie.

"I was nervous before the Clydebank game and Hearts struggled badly," Hearts fan Mike Smith remembered. "I was still nervous after it but I thought that was it. We were starting to look edgy but still weren't losing and there's the old cliché about it being the sign of a good team winning even when they're playing poorly. All those months unbeaten and it just came down to one more game, one more point. I wasn't in any doubt anymore. This was our year."

"The relief when that goal went in was incredible," remembered another Hearts supporter, Bobby Mitchell. "The pubs around the ground were all crammed afterwards and I ended up staying out until closing, which pissed off both my wife...and her brother! He lived in Australia but was still mad about Hearts so phoned me every Saturday night for a match report."

The exhilaration was not confined to the club's long-suffering followers either, as Hearts legend John Robertson recalled. "We were getting excited, there's no doubt about that," he said. "The club hadn't won anything since the early 1960s and the players desperately wanted to be part of the team that brought silverware back to Gorgie Road."

Hearts were four points ahead of Celtic – the only other side with a chance of winning the championship – with only one game of their league season remaining. If they avoided defeat when they visited Dundee's Dens Park they would be champions. Celtic still had to play two games – a rearranged fixture against Motherwell the coming Wednesday and then St Mirren on the final day. Hearts' superior goal difference meant Celtic had to win both their games by an aggregate score of 5-0 and hope Dundee beat the Tynecastle side. The odds were stacked firmly in the Jam Tarts' favour.

What followed was one of the most momentous days in the history of Scottish football, the impact of which would reverberate for decades. May 3rd 1986 would go down in the annals of the national game as a day of unparalleled drama. By the time the sun set that evening a legend had been created and grown men across the resolutely macho central belt had openly cried tears of joy and despair.

A hitherto little-known journeyman pro was about to be elevated to the status of hero at two clubs he had never even played for and folk devil – as reviled as the Prime Minister of the day among the section of society that did not prosper under her leadership – at a third. Football's ability to change lives with the flick of a boot was about to be demonstrated like never before.

Sunday, 27th April 1986

"Trust me, son," said Robert Salmond as he hoisted his seven-year-old progeny upon his shoulders to enjoy an unimpeded view of Hearts captain John Cumming lifting the Scottish League Cup, "there will be many more days like this."

Heart's 1-0 victory over Kilmarnock at Hampden had taken place in 1962. Twenty-four years later Robert's son Alex was now a respected oil economist and rapidly climbing the ranks of the Scottish National Party but further glory for his side had remained as elusive as his party's dream of independence.

But there were now few people in Scotland that didn't believe Salmond's footballing fortunes were about to change. Certainly, none of the nation's football writers believed a Jambo capitulation was likely as they named Hearts' player/assistant manager Sandy Jardine as Footballer of the Year the day after his side's narrow win over Clydebank. Jardine was the first player to win the award with two different clubs, with the latest accolade coming 11 years after his first with Rangers. It was a fitting tribute for the evergreen defender who had played his 1000th professional match in a season that saw him celebrate his 37th birthday.

"Sandy was our player of the year, not just because he'd had a tremendous season but because we all believed he'd inspired his team to a historic and entirely unexpected league title," explained Ron Scott, the estimable *Sunday Post* football writer who has served Scotland's press corps since the late 1960s. "The challenge came from nowhere, it really did. Nobody thought for one minute Hearts were capable of mounting a challenge. It was an incredible story."

Indeed Scott, writing under his nom de plume of Bill McFarlane, had nailed his colours to the mast in that morning's paper. "Celtic still have a fingertip on the League Championship trophy," he wrote. "But surely they are fated to slip off the edge and miss out to Hearts." Having watched the Celts beat Dundee 2-0 at home the day before, the writer berated what he saw as an "unbelievably lethargic" performance given the stakes and the fact visiting forward Ray Stephen had been sent off after only 30 minutes.

While admitting it was still mathematically possible for Celtic to capture the league flag, Scott concluded that "it would be a travesty now if they robbed Hearts at the last gasp."

To stand on the brink of glory as they did was beyond the wildest dreams of even the most ardent Hearts fan. Qualification for Europe was the target at the start of the season but even that was hoped for rather than expected. Finishing in the upper echelons of the Scottish Premier Division or winning a cup competition meant not only going toe to toe with Glasgow giants Celtic and Rangers but also Alex Ferguson's Aberdeen and Jim McLean's Dundee United, upstarts from the north east who had won nine trophies between them over the past few years. City rivals Hibernian, Dundee and St Mirren also harboured realistic ambitions of European football and/or silverware in August 1985.

"It was only three years before that we became a Premier League team again after a terrible period yo-yoing between the divisions," said Jambo Mike Smith. "If you'd asked at the start of the season I would have said a relegation battle was far more likely so to be going into the last game top of the league and favourites to win it was dreamland stuff."

As one of the most competitive seasons in Scottish football history got underway it appeared Hearts would have to downgrade their goal of competing with the Old and New Firms to simply surviving in the top flight. The Jambos' expectations had already been reined in by a decade of of turmoil – both on and off the field – so the club's seventh-place finish in 1984/85, a second successive season of top flight consolidation, was regarded as satisfactory, particularly as it was one spot above their rivals from across the city. Under player-manager Alex 'Doddie' MacDonald, Hearts had been steadily rebuilding and when only an injury-time equaliser from Paul McStay prevented summer signing John Colquhoun from securing an opening day win over the club he had just left, hopes of further progress seemed justified.

This positive – if frustrating and ultimately costly start – seemed to be nothing more than a cruel false dawn when the boys in maroon were brought crashing back to earth by a 6-2 thrashing away to St Mirren the following week. Goals from Colquhoun and Clark bagged a derby win to ensure the bragging rights stayed in Gorgie at the end of August but that was to be the highlight of a poor early season. Hearts took only five points from their first eight league games and languished third from bottom, having already crashed out of the League Cup, leaving the travelling support despondent as they trudged away from a desperate 1-0 defeat at Kilbowie on 28th September. The faithful could take some solace from Hibs propping up the table at this stage but schadenfreude wasn't enough to stop the Jam Tarts peering nervously over their collective shoulders before the season's quarter mark had even been passed.

"We had a shocking start to the season," said Colquhoun in an edition of the BBC series *That Was The Team That Was*. "People were talking about us being relegated rather than challenging for Europe, which was the aim."

"Hearts had a lot of injuries and suspensions early on," recalled Smith. "When the team lost to Aberdeen, Motherwell and Clydebank we were sinking towards the bottom of the league. Only pointless Hibs were sparing us that indignity."

Things were so bad that crisis talks were held in the Tynecastle boardroom, as club owner Wallace Mercer recalled in *TWTTTW*. "Well, I remember sitting with my club secretary after being beaten by Clydebank, scratching my head at the end of the first quarter of the 85/86 season, saying to Les Porteous, 'What are we going to do here?'"

Colquhoun's early-season form was one of the few bright spots for the club and he was well on the way to repaying the £35,000 Hearts shelled out for his services. Having netted four times already, he was Hearts' joint-top scorer when Dundee came to visit the week after the Clydebank debacle. The signs were ominous when the Dark Blues took an early lead but a second-half equaliser from recent signing Iain Jardine was enough to secure a point and stop the rot. Not Jardine, nor his team-mates, manager nor any of the 8512 fans in attendance could have known that point was to herald the start of the most incredible run in the club's 112-year history.

The Saturday following the Dundee game saw an unfancied Hearts travel to the east end of Glasgow to take on top-of-the-table Celtic. Just as they had on the opening day of the season, the Jam Tarts shocked their opponents by taking the lead around the half-hour mark only this time there was to be no late reprieve for the Glasgow giants. Hearts saw the game out for a win that Alex MacDonald believes was the catalyst for their title challenge.

"I felt the actual turning point in our season came when we beat Celtic 1–0 at Parkhead," he said in his autobiography *Doddie*. "The confidence within the team began to soar from then onwards, with consequences none of us could have imagined...having started the season as 200–1 against to win the title, the odds became ever shorter thereafter."

A series of impressive results followed as Hearts began to climb the table. The remainder of October saw St Mirren swept aside 3-0 before a goal from centre-half Craig Levein secured a precious victory over Aberdeen, Hearts' first over Fergie's Dons since MacDonald took over. November yielded three more wins, including a 3-0 trouncing of Rangers in which Sandy Jardine became the first player in Scotland to play 1000 professional games. By the end of the month Hearts had climbed to second in the table but no one was yet talking about them as serious title contenders even though the team was clearly a very different proposition to the side that had started the season.

The introduction of three points for a win was still some years off so back-to-back draws in their next two games were hardly disastrous for the Jambos, particularly as the last of them saw Celtic fail to make up ground on them. The team exorcised the ghost of their previous visit to Love Street in some style when a solitary Kenny Black counter meant St Mirren were not only dispatched but that Hearts were top of the league for the first time in the season. Things were getting serious now and crowds at Tynecastle rose in direct proportion to the excitement that was building around Alex MacDonald's unlikely challengers.

"We just enjoyed our football and never spoke about winning the league because we were as surprised as anyone how things panned out," said Sandy Clark in his autobiography, *From The Heart*. "We were a team and that was our strength. We just kept going and never got carried away."

Clark's manager also said no one dared consider that winning the league was possible for fear they might lose their collective nerve but on the back of a lengthening unbeaten run and with none of the other contenders threatening to break clear of the chasing pack, it was impossible to stop thoughts running ahead to May, as John Robertson acknowledged. "We thought then that we could definitely qualify for Europe and perhaps push all the way for the title," he said.

Alex MacDonald attributed the upturn in his team's fortunes to the partnership that had developed between Sandy Jardine and Craig Levein in central defence, in addition to a conscious effort to improve the side's possession play. The improvement in defence was demonstrated by the fact Hearts were to lose just one goal from a corner the whole season and, in making Hearts harder to play against, their considerable attacking threat was free to wreak havoc across the country.

Two John Colquhoun goals at Ibrox meant Hearts saw out the year in winning style and 1986 saw them pick up where they left off with a 3-1 success in the Ne'er Day derby. Not only had the old enemy been humbled once again but Hearts moved four points clear at the top of the table as the unbeaten run stretched to 14. To the chagrin of all of a Hibee persuasion, as well as Aberdeen, Celtic and United – all sitting two wins behind though still with games in hand – the Jambo juggernaut seemed unstoppable. *West End Girls* had just displaced Shakin' Stevens' *Merry Christmas Everyone* at the top of the charts to claim the first number one spot of 1986. In Edinburgh though, it was 'the west end boys' who were top of the pile.

"The first time I thought 'we can actually do this' was when we took Rangers apart just after Christmas," recalled Mike Smith. "We were top of the league and when we beat Aberdeen at Pittodrie a month later 'we might win the league' became 'we're going to do this'. You obviously have some doubts because this was uncharted territory but the confidence was growing all the time."

The mounting frenzy was also hitting Bobby Mitchell's Sydney-based brother-in-law in the pocket. "When Alan and his family emigrated it used to be a monthly phone call home. Then we started winning a few games and they became more regular. Towards the end of the season it was every Saturday night, which was when he'd got up on the Sunday morning. This was obviously pre-satellite TV and internet so he had the radio and me for info. He wanted to know everything, how so-and-so played, tactics, injuries etc. He had strong opinions on players he'd never seen play. After about 10 minutes my wife would grab the phone only for her big brother to tell her he'd have to go as it was costing him a fortune. She'd ask me about Alan's job, how his wife was and how our nieces were doing at school. I just shrugged. 'Well, what did the two of you talk about for all that time?' 'Sandy Jardine and John Robertson, mainly,' I told her."

Attendances at home were now topping the 20,000 mark on occasion while the ever-increasing maroon army were filling away grounds the length and breadth of Scotland. A capacity crowd of more than 27,000 crammed into Tynecastle for the visit of Rangers on Scottish Cup duty as Hearts' opened up a second front in their quest for glory. An action-packed second-half saw the home team recover from an Ally McCoist opener to record a 3-2 win, the third humbling of the season for the Ibrox giants at the hands of Hearts, to progress to the fourth round.

The remarkable run threatened to come to an end the following week at Kilbowie – scene of Hearts' last reverse way back in October – but Clydebank were left deflated by a late Sandy Clark equaliser as the Jam Tarts simply refused to accept defeat. The side bounced back with a resounding 3-1 win when Dundee visited Tynecastle the following Saturday and a John Robertson leveller at Parkhead the week after ensured Hearts would go the entire season undefeated against one of their main rivals for the title. The result meant Celtic had missed a golden opportunity to close the gap on the league leaders and remained five points adrift, although they had played two games less than Hearts. Aberdeen and United also saw their deficits as eminently bridgeable as both had games in hand over the Jambos. Rangers were, by this time, starting to fall behind the chasing pack and looked more likely to fight it out for the final UEFA Cup berth at best.

Hamilton Academical and St Mirren were dispatched with the minimum of fuss to send Hearts into a Scottish Cup semi-final against Dundee United, while they continued to sweep all before them on league business. Four straight wins saw them defeat Rangers for a fourth time and then break the Gers' record for consecutive Premier Division games unbeaten in the process. Painfully for followers of Edinburgh's other leading club the record was clinched at Easter Road in front of nearly 21,000 fans. Hearts were top of the league with six games to go. They were in the semi-final of the Scottish Cup. They scored goals with regularity and were tight at the back. Seemingly no one was able to find a way of derailing their momentum. Hibees, whose sense of dread had been growing since October, were by now in a state of open despair.

The next test awaiting Hearts was back-to-back meetings with Dundee United. A John Colquhoun counter was enough to earn his side a first Scottish Cup final since 1976 while the league game a week later saw the Jambos comprehensively dismantle a United team containing the bulk of the side that would beat Barcelona home and away on the way to the following season's UEFA Cup final. The 3-0 scoreline was a bitter blow to the Arabs' title hopes. United, Celtic and Aberdeen all still had games in hand to play but none could stop Hearts if the Tynecastle club won their final three games. Now unbeaten in 31 games in all competitions few would have bet against Hearts doing just that.

"Everyone was expecting them to slip up but they just kept going and proving us all wrong," remembered broadcaster and Aberdeen fan Richard Gordon. "They beat us home and away and that was some achievement in those days. Then they went to Tannadice and took apart a very good Dundee United team and then people had to acknowledge they might just be the real deal."

Mike Smith was no less impressed. "The thing is, I wasn't surprised that we beat United but I never expected it to be 3-0. It was an unforgettable afternoon and it seemed the fantasy of Hearts becoming champions was about to become reality. It was the best performance and result yet and a lot of people thought we had won the league that day."

Having lost their last game to Celtic, Aberdeen knew they were drinking in the last chance saloon when they visited Tynecastle on Sunday, 20th April 1986. The game was played on a Sunday to accommodate the cameras recording the first-ever Scottish league match to be screened live on television. This unprecedented exposure was in stark contrast to a dispute over money between broadcasters and the football authorities that had resulted in no football being televised between September and March. The arrangement was not entirely to the satisfaction of Hearts' manager Alex MacDonald, as he made clear in *Doddie*: "Our feeling was that the added hype might get to our players who, after all, were far less used to being the focus of the nation's attention than Aberdeen."

"Our players, many of whom weren't used to the intensity of pressure that comes with chasing titles, didn't need the extra burden of playing to a big television audience for the first time," agreed his assistant in *Score and More: The Sandy Jardine Story*. "Under the circumstances, it wasn't surprising that we didn't play particularly well."

The live event was no classic for the armchair viewer. A Peter Weir penalty gave the visitors the lead as the match entered its closing stages but this Hearts side had a spirit and a will-to-win instilled by their management team that had seen them through battle after battle during the season. Once again, maroon sleeves were rolled up, teeth gritted and defeat refused to be countenanced. Just five minutes after Aberdeen took the lead, John Robertson poked the ball into the net to spark scenes of wild abandon on the Tynecastle terraces.

As Hearts' challengers fell by the wayside, the numbers willing the underdog to go all the way grew, as Richard Gordon remembered. "Even before that Tynecastle match it was clear to me that we wouldn't be winning the league. I definitely wanted Hearts to win it and I didn't for a second doubt they would do it from there. I think most fans of other teams had got behind them by that point and wanted them to win it rather than Celtic."

Notable exceptions to this were the followers of Hibernian. What would normally be seen as a forgettable season looked certain to become unforgettable for all the wrong reasons, according to Hibee John Craig. "I didn't really pay the situation too much attention to begin with because we didn't expect the unbeaten run to last. You were still expecting them to slip up but they never did. Then they went to Tannadice and I thought to myself, 'they could win this'. It came to the Aberdeen match on the Sunday live on TV and you were thinking 'this is it'. When they got a draw to keep the unbeaten run going I felt that was the last opportunity of them slipping up gone. I was resigned to them winning the league after that."

And so Hearts' tilt at glory came down to two games against Clydebank and Dundee – both teams who had caused them problems over the season. With relegation suspended due to league reconstruction, there was nothing but pride at stake for the bottom-placed Bankies when they visited the home of the team at the opposite end of the table. The 1-0 victory meant Hearts had completed the league season without losing at home, with Sandy Jardine acknowledging that Hearts' form at Tynecastle had been the basis for a title challenge that was attracting attention far away from Gorgie.

"I think Hearts had captured the imagination of football supporters everywhere that season," wrote Jardine in his autobiography. "As the number of unbeaten games kept totting up week by week we found there was interest in our exploits from as far apart as Canada and the USA, Australia and New Zealand, as well as throughout Europe."

One hurdle, in the shape of a team they had proven themselves to be a better side than over the course of the season, remained. Hearts had momentum and, increasingly it seemed, destiny on their side. They didn't even need to leave Dens Park with full points. A draw would be enough. Just avoid defeat – as they had done 31 times in a row – and they would be champions.

A team of which so little had been expected was within touching distance of one of the biggest achievements in Scottish sporting history and the nation was gripped by the drama. This was not just a club reborn but one whose miracles had captured the imagination of the country. All but the supporters of Celtic, Hibernian and Dundee appeared desperate for the underdog to win out on the final day.

Glory was tantalisingly close and, as it always does in the build up to momentous occasions, thoughts turned to who would emerge as the hero of the day and write their name in the history books.

Monday, 28th April 1986

"World Cup warm-up a shambles" cried out the day's *Glasgow Herald* headline as a traumatic campaign saw the national team limp towards Mexico and Scotland's fourth consecutive World Cup finals.

Tragedy is often glibly used in football but there was no other way to describe what had happened the night Scotland played Wales in Cardiff the previous September. Wales needed to win to keep their hopes of qualification alive while a draw would be enough for Scotland to earn a play-off against Australia. The hour-mark had just passed and the hosts were 1-0 up when Scotland manager Jock Stein threw Davie Cooper into the fray in place of Gordon Strachan. The Rangers winger subsequently equalised from the penalty spot but the decision to bring him on was to prove the last of Stein's life. He collapsed on the trackside shortly before the end of the game and was rushed inside the stadium's medical room for emergency treatment. Despite the best efforts of the Ninian Park medical staff, the man many considered to be the greatest ever Scottish manager succumbed to heart failure and died at the age of 62.

Stein's assistant was Alex Ferguson and the Aberdeen boss, though utterly distraught at the loss of his friend and mentor, agreed to take the manager's job on a temporary basis. The passing of 'Big Jock' cast a long shadow over the whole of Scottish football but Ferguson managed to galvanise the national side and emerge triumphant from the play-off, winning 2-0 on aggregate. The Australia games, which took place in November and December 1985 would also have unintended consequences for the domestic season.

The logistics of getting the Scottish squad to and from Australia resulted in two weeks when the Premier League fixture list was almost entirely depleted in early December, just as Hearts were hitting their stride. Despite the exceptional run they embarked upon, the Tynecastle squad remained untroubled by international recognition. The December postponements, combined with weather-related call-offs, meant the second half of the season was marked by speculation about the implications of games in hand for the chasing pack. Hearts were also the only one of the sides who occupied the top-five spots for the majority of the season not to have qualified for Europe the previous season. This and a fortunate run with injury and suspension meant there had been less strain on Alex MacDonald's playing staff than the others.

"Consistency of selection was a big help," he noted in *Doddie*. "I liked nothing better than to say to players in the dressing room before a game, 'Same team as last Saturday'."

Celtic's superior financial resources meant they should have been better equipped to deal with any manpower crisis resulting from injury, illness or suspension, but there was little they could do about the circumstances leading to the late-season fixture congestion that manager Davie Hay and the club's supporters were left bitterly angry about.

The Parkhead club's penultimate match of the season had originally been scheduled to take place on the same day as Hearts' meeting with Clydebank at Tynecastle. As planned, they played Dundee that day but there was still the matter of their oft-postponed visit to Fir Park to deal with a few days later.

The two sides had originally been due to meet on 1st March, but a series of call-offs meant the final midweek of the season was the last available date for the game to be played. The Scottish Football League were determined that under no circumstances would any fixtures be played beyond the designated final day of the league season but this meant a clash with Scotland's World Cup warm-up match against Holland in Eindhoven on the Tuesday of that week. Motherwell were also insistent that the game be played before the Dundee-Hearts encounter as Celtic remaining in contention would ensure a bumper gate at Fir Park. The result was an unseemly spat that left Celtic supporters, not for the first or last time, to claim the authorities were determined to do everything in their power to undermine the Parkhead side's on-field endeavours.

Regardless of whether or not there was any substance behind the claims, Celtic reacted to the selection of Paul McStay, Roy Aitken and Murdo MacLeod by refusing to release three of their biggest stars for the game. Ferguson was exasperated that such a situation could arise on the eve of the final friendly before the World Cup squad was announced. His short tenure with Scotland had already given him a taste of the frustrations that Stein had endured and that would no doubt await his successor. A slew of top players frequently called off for international duty and had their commitment to the Scotland cause questioned while the announcement of each squad seemed to bring a fresh club versus country row.

Given the importance of the Motherwell match it is difficult to imagine any club reacting differently to how Celtic did and, while the Scottish Football League's reluctance to diminish the showpiece finale of a remarkable season was also far from unreasonable, conflict was inevitable. The situation was descending into farce with the SFL suggesting the Celtic trio be allowed to fly back from Holland early after the game to enable them to play in the Motherwell match, which would be moved from the Wednesday to Thursday evening.

The proposal was given short shrift, as Celtic director Jack McGinn, explained in Monday's *Glasgow Herald*. "If the Celtic players had to play on Tuesday, Thursday and Saturday, Hearts made a mess of it, and we failed to cash in, where would we stand with our fans? They would think we were headcases."

Ferguson had been told Celtic couldn't withdraw their players the previous Thursday, only to be told by Davie Hay later the same day that the Celtic boss intended to do exactly that. At the same time, the Scottish Football Association continued to insist there would be no withdrawal as Celtic could cancel their game with three players called-up. This stance, however, failed to take into account the reluctance of Motherwell or the SFL to rearrange the fixture. The national team boss expressed sympathy for Celtic before saying, "It's this situation that all Scottish managers are faced with...the Dutch will be wondering what kind of country we are but we will just need to bite the bullet and get on with it."

In the end, Rangers' Ally Dawson, Dundee's Bobby Connor and Gary Mackay of Hearts were called up to the squad as replacements and flew to Holland on the last Monday of April, leaving the *Glasgow Herald*'s Jim Reynolds to comment that: "In yet another club versus country confrontation – not to mention mix-up between the Scottish league and Scottish Football Association – Scotland are here with a shadow squad and because of it Celtic players could find their World Cup places in jeopardy."

Hoops gaffer Davie Hay was defiant: "I don't care what anyone says, Celtic are blameless. In fact, we have bent over backwards to help Scotland, Mother-well and everyone else. We were prepared to leave the game until next week when there would have been no problem but the League ordered the match to go ahead."

One of the players unwittingly caught up in the drama was also in no doubt about where his loyalties lay. "You want to play for your country, you really do," said Murdo MacLeod. "It is a really special experience and if there was an international coming up then I wanted to be there but the priority is winning the league for your club. With games coming up that could see us win the title that's all I was focusing on."

MacLeod and Hay were certainly more confident of Celtic's chances than most. Already grieving for the loss of their legendary manager, Celtic fans were all but resigned to one of the most difficult seasons in their history petering out without silverware to dedicate to the memory of Stein.

"For Celtic the finishing line is all too close and it

appears Hearts will not be overtaken," wrote future *Guardian* chief football writer and author of several Celtic books Kevin McCarra in the final days of 1985/86. "No matter what, Celtic will not look back on this season with pleasure."

"As I was getting older and thinking about things more it did start to occur to me that Celtic were in terminal decline," wrote Celtic fan Paul Larkin in his book, *Albert, Dougie and Wim*, demonstrating how McCarra's unflinching summary was a view widely shared by fans and pundits alike.

Having crashed out of the League Cup on penalties to Hibernian earlier in the season, Celtic were stunned when a frantic end to an exhilarating Scottish Cup quarter final at Easter Road meant the same opponents had eliminated them at the same stage of both knock-out competitions and at the same venue. The fact that the sides had produced two of the most entertaining cup ties of this or any other season was of little consolation to the Celtic faithful, for whom the 4-4 and 4-3 scorelines painfully illustrated the defensive frailties that had been apparent since August. Without a Miller and McLeish, a Narey and Hegarty or even a Levein and Jardine keeping things tight at the back, Celtic had relied on their considerable firepower to stay in touch with their fellow contenders. They had spent just two weeks at the league's summit the whole season and sat in fifth place at Christmas. When they occupied that position once more in mid-January, level on points with their Old Firm rivals, it appeared that if the league title was not destined for Gorgie, then it would be taking up residence in Dundee or Aberdeen come May.

"I remember Hearts sitting top of the table at the turn of the year building up a lead while we built up games in hand," said Murdo MacLeod. "They were winning big games at that time, taking full points but we were still thinking they would fall away. They will lose a couple of games and that would be that, but they didn't. I always believe that you never win the medals in January and that if you keep going you'll have a chance at the end of the season because you never know what will happen and there are always twists and turns. We thought it was always possible to catch them because we expected them to drop points but they kept winning games when we weren't playing. Seeing the size of the gap grow, even with the other teams having games in hand, would have been a massive boost for them."

With Hearts four points ahead of them having completed 35 of their 36 league fixtures, Celtic faced an uphill battle if they were to avoid finishing the season without a trophy. Maximum points and several goals were required from their two remaining matches but even that depended on their rivals losing at Dundee. It appeared the good form Celtic had shown in the second half of the season had come too late.

"It wasn't that Celtic were bad that year but there hadn't really been anything notable throughout the season," remembered lifelong fan and former Celtic Supporters' Association Secretary Eddie Toner. "It didn't look like Hearts would ever slip up. If you saw someone listening to the radio in the crowd it got to the stage where we only asked for the Rangers score because we expected Hearts to win. And we never seemed to be pegging them back to any great extent. We couldn't expect anyone to do us a favour unless we did our part ourselves and maybe heap a bit more pressure on Hearts."

With talent like MacLeod, Danny McGrain, Roy Aitken, Tommy Burns, Paul McStay, Maurice Johnston and Brian McClair at Davie Hay's disposal, Toner's belief that Celtic had been underwhelming rather than inadequate bears up to scrutiny. In fairness to Hay, the gap at the top of the table had always been exaggerated by Hearts having played more games than their challengers and Celtic had shown remarkable consistency against the Premier League's lesser lights, dropping only three points against teams in the bottom-half of the table all season. In contrast, the Celts had failed to beat Hearts in four attempts and suffered three defeats at the hands of Dundee United, two to Aberdeen and one to Rangers. Thirty-three of their points so far had been accumulated in games against the bottom five and only 17 against the other top-half sides. While the Jambos were winning over neutrals with swashbuckling displays like the 3-0 win at Tannadice, beating both sides of the Old Firm in Glasgow and defeating the mighty Aberdeen home and away, Celtic had kept in touch in a relatively mundane manner.

That their challenge lacked the romance and drama of Heart's title charge was of little concern to Hay, his players or anyone of a Celtic persuasion. They knew the odds were against them but could only play the cards they had been dealt and hope for what most believed would amount to a miracle. And while most of the country had by now thrown their weight behind Hearts, there were also those who had allied themselves with Celtic for reasons of naked self-preservation.

Tuesday, 29th April 1986

For Hibernian supporters, season 1985/86 could scarcely have gone worse. As the term approached its conclusion, Hearts were on course for a league and cup double just as the Easter Road side were struggling to come to terms with the sale of star striker Gordon Durie to Chelsea for a record £400,000 coming as it did less than six months after the tragic death of club legend Erich Schaedler.

'Shades', then playing for Dumbarton, was found in his car in the Cardrona Forest on Christmas Eve 1985 with a single shotgun wound to the head. His death was recorded as suicide although members of the former Scotland cap's family maintain unanswered questions surround the incident and believe he may have been the victim of foul play.

It was not just fans of Schaedler's current and former clubs that were left reeling from the news. Across Scotland, people were stunned not just by the loss of a high-profile footballer but by the circumstances surrounding the death of a popular and apparently happy young man. Coming just months after the passing of Jock Stein, Scottish football was plunged into mourning once again.

Schaedler had only joined Dumbarton that summer following a second spell at Hibs. In his first, the left-back had been a hugely popular member of 'Turnbull's Tornadoes', the Hibs team that ran Celtic close for the league title, competed in Scottish Cup finals, won the League Cup and two Drybrough Cups and drubbed Hearts 7-0. The early 1970s seemed a long time ago to Hibees.

"What happened to Shades – I couldn't believe it. He'd still been playing for us a few months earlier. You shout abuse at footballers or sing their name and think they're somehow different to the rest of us because of the job they do, then something like that happens," said Hibs fan Colin Christie. "Everyone was shocked and I mean everyone in Scottish football, not just Hibees. You try to keep football and real life separate and something like that should keep things in perspective but I'm not proud of the fact Hearts going on that run made me feel worse. Durie was sold and even though we got good money for him it was all starting to feel like there was no point."

Despite being one of the clubs expected to benefit from the mid-1970s league reorganisation, Hibs hadn't found the new top-10 format to be particularly kind to them. The first season of the Premier Division in 1975/76 saw the Easter Road side finish a respectable third, a position they were not to match for almost two decades. By the mid-80s Hibs were regularly found languishing in the bottom half of the league, as likely to be drawn into a relegation battle as to challenge for Europe. They had, however, spent just a solitary season outside the top division while Hearts had suffered three relegations since reconstruction. Having lifted silverware a decade more recently than Hearts and with European exploits and a 7-0 thrashing of their city rivals to look back on fondly, Hibs fans would certainly have felt that the recent history of Edinburgh football belonged to them prior to Alex MacDonald's arrival at Tynecastle.

Hearts were about to finish above their rivals for the third season in a row. Hibs had failed to win any of the 12 derbies played in that time, losing six and drawing six, but even that would pale into insignificance if the Jambos went on to do what most of the country was now willing them to do. For Hibs' fans in the first part of Thatcher's decade, Hearts never winning another title or cup seemed a reasonably realistic proposition. But as April gave way to May, the doomsday scenario of them doing both, in the same season and at a time when their own side's fortunes were on a downward trajectory, drew ever closer.

Hope certainly did not spring eternal for Hibee John Craig. "In the week running up to the game my mood didn't shift. I was resigned to it. There was absolutely no way they would slip up now. The league was theirs. Dundee at Dens shouldn't have been a foregone conclusion but when you looked at the run Hearts had been on you didn't think Dundee would beat them when no one else could manage it. Not only that but Celtic had to win well at St Mirren. The whole thing seemed impossible.

"It didn't actually matter what Celtic did as, in my head, there had been no doubt Hearts would do it themselves from the Aberdeen game onwards. I was just wishing it was over by that stage. I knew they would win the league and I was trying not to think about it too much."

And yet, just six months earlier it appeared more likely that the end of Edinburgh's trophy drought would be celebrated in Leith rather than Gorgie. Following their dramatic League Cup victory against Celtic, Hibs took on the other side of the Old Firm in a two-legged semi-final. The 2-0 lead they took into the second leg was to prove enough for Hibs as Rangers could only manage a single goal in front of their own fans. Backed by a 20,000-strong green-and-white army, Hibernian headed to Hampden in late October hoping to deny Alex Ferguson a first League Cup trophy.

Despite league titles and Scottish Cups galore in the early part of the 1980s, Aberdeen had twice missed out on success in the third of Scotland's major honours during Ferguson's reign. With a clean sweep now within their grasp and a demanding gaffer to placate, the Dons were in no mood to show mercy to a patently inferior Hibs team and ran out comfortable 3-0 winners.

Richard Gordon was one of the celebrating Aberdeen fans that day and says there had been little doubt in his mind going into the game about the outcome. "We got to the final having not conceded a goal and having beaten Dundee United home and away in the semi. There was an extra edge as it was the one trophy that had eluded Fergie. He'd won three leagues, four Scottish Cups, the Cup-Winners Cup and European Super Cup, but he'd never managed to win the League Cup so winning that meant a lot to him, the team and fans. We actually lost the first three finals under Ferguson then won every time we reached the final after that. There had been a couple of horrible exits in that competition so this was our chance to put all that right and by that time in Ferguson's reign, we won finals if we got to them."

"Aberdeen were just too good for us in the final," agreed John Craig. "We were never in the game. It was disappointing because the wins over Celtic on penalties and Rangers in the semi-final over two legs were brilliant. At the start of the season I was confident we'd be a wee bit better than the season before because we had a few really good players. I thought we could maybe challenge for Europe and get a decent cup run. Even though we got to the final and they didn't, there was inevitable stick from the Jambos afterwards."

Jambo Mike Smith, then living in the Granite City, found himself aligned with his fellow residents for once. "It was pretty insufferable living in Aberdeen in the 1980s because they were winning everything and letting you know all about it but I was on their side that day. To be honest, I was never that worried as Aberdeen were so good but I always enjoy the Hibees getting beat! I wouldn't say I was envious as even at that stage it was clear we had a better team than them but I do remember thinking how good it would be to be reaching cup finals and how we should be aiming to challenge the top teams as well."

Disappointed by their Hampden flop as they were, Hibees could at least take comfort from the unlikelihood of their rivals heaping more misery upon them beyond the taunts, winks and jokes that Jambos greeted their return with. With Hearts just three games into their remarkable unbeaten run, the other side of the city appeared to pose little danger at this stage. Hibs sat just two points behind Hearts in a league table they looked as likely to climb. Replicating their impressive cup form in the league was uppermost in the minds of Hibs supporters and players. Reversing a desperate run of derby results was all they worried about as far as Hearts were concerned.

The knock-out competitions were to prove the only high points of John Blackley's last full season as Hibernian manager. Dunfermline and Ayr United were dealt with before Hibs squeezed past Celtic by the odd goal in seven in the classic Scottish Cup quarter-final. The mouth-watering prospect of an all-Edinburgh Scottish Cup Final briefly appeared on the horizon but, while Hearts were taking care of Dundee United, another 3-0 thumping from Aberdeen meant Hibs' wait for a Scottish Cup win, then stretching to 84 years, went on.

As they approached the final fixture, a visit from Dundee United, Hibs knew the highest they could finish was eighth. A trio of losses to Hearts through-out the season brought further frustration to the Hibs faithful, whose side had missed the opportunity to inflict a body blow on the title favourites with just six games remaining. Sandy Clark opened the scoring for Hearts in the first half but a 64th minute equal-iser from Steve Cowan gave Hibees hope of offering the chasing pack the chance make inroads into the Jambos lead at the top. The home supporters on the Easter Road terraces were still dancing and taunting the silenced enemy that lay across the segregation fences when boyhood Hibs fan John Robertson grabbed the winner for Hearts. Fate appeared to be firmly on Hearts' side whilst conspiring against their city rivals.

As Murdo MacLeod made clear when discussing his call-up wrangle, club ultimately came before country for most footballers and supporters were even more certain in their priorities. Given the fact that the destination of that season's league title could be decided in as little as 24 hours hence, Scotland's friendly in Eindhoven was unlikely to prove much of a distraction for anyone with an emotional investment in Heart of Midlothian, Hibernian, Celtic or Rangers. The Holland match came a week after a 2-1 defeat at the hands of England at Wembley, Ferguson's first reversal since taking charge on an interim basis, and the patched-up Scots could consider themselves unlucky to have drawn the game 0-0.

Dundee's Bobby Connor and Ally McCoist of Rangers made their full international debuts in Eindhoven. The Dutch had goalkeeper Hans van Breukelen and Austrian referee Helmut Kohl, who turned down two strong Scottish penalty claims, to thank for the scoreline remaining blank. With Rinus Michel's side containing the likes of van Breukelen, Danny Blind, Ronald Koeman, Adri van Tiggelen, Jan Wouters, Gerald Vanenburg, John van 't Schip and John Bosman – many of whom would star as the Netherlands won the European Championships two years later – the signs for Scotland looked promising ahead of Mexico.

"It was a tremendous result in the circumstances," said Scots manager Ferguson. "I was delighted with every one of them. I thought we should have won and could have had a couple of penalties."

Turning to new caps Connor and McCoist, he added, "It's a good chance to find out if they are indeed international class. After the World Cup, it will be someone else's job to decide. I'm too young for the job."

It was the clearest indication yet that the Aberdeen manager had no interest in becoming national boss on a permanent, full-time basis. While the scale of

Ferguson's ambitions in club football were well known, the bureaucracy and politics he was forced to deal with – illustrated by the 'SFA to investigate warm-up farce' headlines in that morning's newspapers – could hardly have endeared him to the role either.

Aberdeen fans, who had already seen Ferguson reject overtures from Rangers, Wolverhampton Wanderers, Tottenham Hotspur and Arsenal, and who braced themselves for the inevitable speculation whenever a high-profile managerial vacancy opened up, could breathe a sigh of relief. For the moment at least.

Wednesday, 30th April 1986

Nineteen-eighty-six was the year that the world first became acquainted with the previously alien concept of the PC virus. 'Brain' erased memory, slowed hard drives and quickly spread around the world. It was a watershed moment in the history of technology but a rather more prosaic and old-fashioned virus was causing concern to the Hearts management team 72 hours before the biggest game in the club's history.

John Colquhoun, Neil Berry and Kenny Black had fallen victim to a flu bug at the start of the week and were told to stay away from Tynecastle for a few days to try and contain the infection. For Alex MacDonald and Sandy Jardine, trying to protect their players from pressure inevitable in the build up to a match of such magnitude, it was a relief when all three players reported for training on the Wednesday.

"Publicly, our approach remained low-key," Jardine said in *Score and More*. "But behind the scenes the week began badly. It had been so long since we'd had any problems with injuries or illness that the timing of the drama couldn't have been more inopportune."

Hearts fans knew nothing of the immunological problems MacDonald and Jardine were forced to contend with. Wisely, given the air of anticipation surrounding the fixture, the duo decided to keep the problem to themselves in the hope that – like the virus – the news wouldn't spread and the scare would pass without impacting upon their approach or giving Celtic renewed hope of an upset at Dens.

Hearts supporter Mike Smith had other medical matters to concern him that midweek. "My wife was expecting our first child just a week later so I was in ecstatic mood anyway as the season drew to a close," he said. "Then as we got closer to both big dates, self-ishly I was thinking 'what if the wife goes early? Am I going to miss Hearts winning the league here?'"

There, of course, remained the possibility that the title would be surrendered by Celtic before then. Hearts fans had watched the Celtic-Scotland saga unfold, wondering whether McStay, MacLeod and Aitken would be in their usual places at Fir Park and, if they were, what effect the dispute would have on the Celtic team. No doubt some had mixed feelings as the kick-off approached, desperate to have their historic title wrapped up as soon as possible but also preferring for the coronation to be delayed so Hearts could clinch it on their own merit at Dens Park on Saturday.

"There was still a chance that Celtic would drop points in midweek but I was hoping we would be allowed to win the league for ourselves at the week-end," said Hearts fan Bobby Mitchell. "There was a real bond between the players and the fans. I've never known togetherness like that. It grew throughout the run. We wanted to win it together."

Across the land, there seemed little doubt that an away victory at Motherwell would only postpone the inevitable. "If Motherwell manage to do what has proved impossible for them so far this season and take at least a point off Celtic the race to the premier division title will be lost and won," said *Glasgow Herald* journalist James Traynor, who added "the real hard part is that Hearts must lose to Dundee" and that "the Tynecastle club could start their celebrations just now and not many would argue."

One man who may have taken issue with his team being written off was Celtic supporter Eddie Toner, though he admits he was exceptional, even among his fellow fans, in that regard. On that Wednesday Eddie, as had become something of a habit for him of late, was emerging from various turf accountants in Glasgow's Dennistoun area with more betting slips bearing the words 'Celtic to win the league' to add to his collection.

"I was still feeling that we were going to do it but I was in the minority of Celtic fans," he said. "In those days I liked a punt on the horses and every time I got a couple of quid back I'd put it on Celtic to win the league at 6/1 or whatever daft odds the bookie was giving. I just thought we had a chance and enough about us to score the goals we needed in the last few games so it was down to Dundee doing us a favour."

Going into the game, Celtic knew they needed to not only win but make significant inroads into the six-goal edge Hearts had in goal difference. As the league's top goalscorers and with the likes of Brian McClair and Maurice Johnston to call upon, finding the net was not a problem but even though the side was no longer haemorrhaging goals like they had earlier in the season, they remained vulnerable at the back. Going all-out in attack played to Celtic's strengths but they had goalkeeper Pat Bonner to thank for a McClair brace being the difference between the two teams come full time, much to the disappointment of Hearts striker Sandy Clark who could see the Fir Park floodlights from the window of his house in nearby Hamilton but who still tried to avoid finding out the result. Curiosity eventually got the better of Clark and he turned on the radio only to find the news was not what he wanted to hear. "The good thing was that the league still remained in our hands," he acknowledged. "If we won it didn't matter what happened to Celtic in Paisley."

"After we beat Clydebank we hatched plans to go to the boozer and listen to Celtic at Fir Park on the Wednesday," said Ian Proudfoot, a Jambo interviewed by Paul Larkin for *Albert, Dougie and Wim*. "They were four points behind us then and any slip up meant we would be champions. We had to put the champagne on ice but we were happy that Celtic didn't score loads there."

The country's papers believed Celtic would come to see the Motherwell match as a missed opportunity. Ian Paul of the *Glasgow Herald* reported that "Celtic made certain that Hearts must write the last chapter of their own astonishing season" while his colleague Jack Adams of the *Daily Record* reflected on "a chance they threw away to give their goals total a real boost. They brought their points total against Motherwell to eight out of eight – and could have scored that number of goals with a bit more patience and guile."

As the only way Celtic could win the league was on goal difference, every single decision was subject to extra scrutiny and some fans questioned whether referee McCluskey's decision to turn down two strong penalty appeals was further evidence that they were victims of a conspiracy. In his post-match press conference, Davie Hay didn't address the penalty claims but remained bullish about his side's title chances. "I feel we should have scored a few more goals and we certainly made the chances. However, I know we will win against St Mirren and the way we are playing we are capable of making the chances to get the target we need."

If the 31 games Hearts had gone without defeat since their Clydebank nadir back in October was breathtaking and absorbing, then the 15-match unbeaten run Celtic had put together in the league was merely impressive. As the dust settled on the controversial Fir Park encounter, Kevin McCarra sat down to write the appraisal of Celtic's season that would appear in the match programme for the Love Street showdown. In it he reflected on how their recent results had caused them to rue the team's earlier inconsistency all the more. The Motherwell win was Celtic's seventh in succession as they grasped the opportunity their games in hand afforded them but still their destiny lay in Hearts' hands. Celtic may have gone 360 minutes without conceding but the weaknesses of earlier in the season – including the loss of 10 goals in successive matches against Aberdeen, United and Rangers – continued to haunt them and made the task they faced at St Mirren all the more daunting.

"The Old Firm are not the force in the land they once were," reflected the *Sunday Post* the day after Rangers and Celtic shared eight goals and two points in an epic derby that marked the end of Scottish football's TV blackout. "Scottish honours look set to evade both Ibrox and Celtic Park for the first time in 31 years."

Indeed, such was the extent of their traditional dominance, were Hearts to secure the title they were overwhelming favourites to win, it would be only the second time since the introduction of the League Cup at the end of World War II that both sides of the Old Firm would finish a season without a trophy. Hearts, Hibs, Aberdeen, both Dundee clubs and Kilmarnock may have upset Scottish football's dynastic natural order on occasion but 27 of the 39 post-war league championships had still been won by the Glasgow giants.

For Aberdeen and Dundee United to have broken the stranglehold of Rangers and Celtic was remarkable. For a third non-Old Firm side in just four years to be on the brink of clinching the championship was unprecedented. For the team threatening to surpass not just Rangers and Celtic but also the very strong sides from the north east to be Hearts was scarcely believable.

Despite being traditionally one of the biggest clubs in Scotland, Hearts had been in decline since they had last seriously challenged for silverware in the mid-1960s. The switch to a smaller top tier was suffocating for several sides and with 20 per cent of the Premier Division relegated the league system was unforgiving for anyone who suffered a bad season. Having got stuck in a relegation-promotion-relegation loop, Hearts were facing a third spell in the First Division and an uncertain future when millionaire businessman Wallace Mercer took over the club in 1981.

"The club had yet again been relegated," remembered Mercer on the 20th anniversary of Hearts' title bid. "They had gone through this yo-yo process and the quality of staff was pretty poor. Any players of any quality had left the club so the whole business had to be built back up again. The club was within days of closure. We'd rescued it from dire, dire straits and our intention at that stage was simply to try and retain an element of full-time football at Tynecastle."

Mercer famously called a series of press conferences on the flimsiest of pretexts in order to raise the club's profile and make sure lapsed and potential supporters could not ignore the revolution he was intent on launching. The chairman could not have been accused of lacking substance to back up his style, however, and he overhauled the club's off-field operations, making it a far more professional and financially viable outfit.

Whatever business and marketing acumen Mercer brought to Hearts, it was the decision to promote club captain Alex MacDonald to the role of player/manager that was to prove his masterstroke. The ill-fated and short-lived managerial reign of Tony Ford had seen Hearts humiliated at home by East Stirlingshire in the League Cup and slip to fifth position in the First Division. MacDonald immediately went about instilling discipline in the dressing room as he sought to stablise the club. By the end of the season they were to miss out on promotion by a single point but the manager built on his promising start the following term. Although Hearts missed out on the 1982/83 title to St Johnstone, they were promoted to the Premier Division as runners-up. With MacDonald in charge and building for the future, Hearts were to avoid the immediate relegation that had plagued them in the past.

Any time a provincial club had succeeded in breaking the Old Firm duopoly it was largely down to the remarkable managerial talent at the helm. The likes of Tommy Wallace, Dave Halliday, Bob Shankly, Willie Waddell, Alex Ferguson and Jim McLean had all built their team from scratch, fine-tuning its style of play, bringing through young talent and dealing shrewdly in the transfer market. 'Doddie' was no different.

MacDonald may have been of unimposing stature but his heart was almost too big for a 5'7" frame that appeared to be carved of pure granite and he is spoken about in reverential tones by the players he earned the undying loyalty of. Statistical analysis, progressive tactics and sports science were not things Alex MacDonald overly concerned himself with. His approach was based around man-management and team spirit. He expected his players to be fitter than their opponents and to win individual battles all over the park. If they did that then they stayed in the team and so long as the points continued to roll in, the squad were allowed a certain amount of licence.

"Alex MacDonald just kept things simple," explained Sandy Clark. "All in all, some weeks we were lucky to do six hours of training. We enjoyed our nights out and daily trips to the burger van, but when it was time to work on the training pitch and in the matches we always gave our all."

His former manager backs up the sentiment in a succinct manner that neatly sums up his entire footballing philosophy. "We drank as a team, we ate as a team, we had fun as a team and occasionally we cried as a team."

After bringing in former Ibrox team-mate Sandy

Jardine as assistant, MacDonald bolstered his squad by bringing in experienced pros to complement the ability of youngsters like John Robertson and Gary Mackay. With money still tight, the lower leagues were raided for rough diamonds like Craig Levein while MacDonald managed to persuade Mercer to loosen the purse strings enough to bring in another former Ger in the shape of Sandy Clark. John Colquhoun was to prove the final piece in the Jambos jigsaw and with a mix of youth and experience willing to run through walls for their manager, the boys in maroon were the talk of the toon once more.

"What Alex MacDonald did for a young manager with limited resources, playing and financial, was incredible," said Ron Scott admiringly. "He built a wonderful team spirit and had a great way with players. He was a great wind-up merchant and the players never knew if he was joking with them or not but it kept them on their toes and they loved him. The chairman as well was never slow to show his appreciation for the players' efforts. Half the time I'm sure they were getting bonuses they didn't know they were on."

After going thirty-one games without defeat and requiring only a point against a mid-table team that hadn't beaten them in three attempts that season, Hearts were not so much title favourites as stick-on certainties. But in the days approaching the Dens Park showdown the presence of a 21-year-old ghost began to loom large in the minds of Jambos as Hibees harked back to events that had gone down in folklore and provided them with much-needed ammunition to fire at their rivals in a desperate attempt to convince themselves that all was not lost.

Kilmarnock had travelled to Tynecastle on the final day of the 1964/65 season trailing Hearts by two points in the title race. Due to the quirks of the goal average system (goals scored divided by goals conceded) used at the time to separate teams tied on points, Killie knew a 2-0 winning scoreline would be enough to give them the title. They achieved it with two first-half strikes and withstood a late Hearts barrage to win the league by 0.04 of a goal.

That the 'decimal decider' was one of the most dramatic occasions in British football history was of little consolation to the disconsolate Jambos, who had scored 90 goals over the season to Kilmarnock's 62 and who had conceded only 16 more than the champions. Bizarrely, another two-goal winning margin for Kilmarnock such as 3-1 or 4-2 would have seen Hearts crowned league winners. Fired up by this perceived injustice, the Tynecastle club petitioned the Scottish Football League to abolish goal average in favour of goal difference, a system that would eventually be introduced a few years later.

The damage had been done, however, and the stunned club entered its long period of decline that was only arrested with the arrival of Mercer and appointment of MacDonald. Now, 21 years later, atonement was finally in sight for Hearts. All the same, as the big day approached, Jambos of a more nervous disposition begin to fear the lightening that probability told them couldn't strike twice.

Celtic fans, though spoiled by success in comparison with their Jambo counterparts, did not have to hark back two decades to remember last-day title disappointment. The Parkhead side had been runners-up in each of the past three years. Although the two previous seasons had seen them finish some distance behind Aberdeen, 1982-83 had seen the Celts go into their final game with a real chance of winning the title.

Unusually, two of Scotland's three city derbies were scheduled to bring the curtain down on the term, meaning the Premier Division's top two both had the chance to win the league on the home turf of their main rivals. Dundee United went into their showdown at Dens Park a point ahead of Celtic and a goal difference superior by a slender two. Aberdeen were also level with Celtic on 53 points but their goal difference was another five worse off so the Dons needed both to drop points while rattling up a cricket score against Hibs as an insurance policy.

To the horror of the Celtic support crammed into three sides of Ibrox, both United and Rangers raced to two-goal leads although news of Dundee pulling one back before the half-hour mark helped lift their spirits slightly. Fired up by manager Billy McNeil's half-time team talk and as determined to say they had at least done their bit as Rangers were to deny their enemy, Celtic blew their hosts away in the second half. The four goals they scored meant a Dundee equaliser would leave United and Celtic tied on points having scored and conceded the exact same number of goals. A leveller 80 miles east and a late fifth for their own side would mean one of the most dramatic and joyous occasions in their history but neither arrived. United were champions for the first time in their history and their fans and players partied at the home of their historic foes while Celtic's brave showing earned them no more than an emotional salute from their supporters and derision from the few Rangers fans who had braved the game to its conclusion.

In Celtic's favour was the fact they didn't have a bruising Old Firm test to pass this time around and, having taken five points from their three encounters with St Mirren so far that season they went into the game confident of a win against a side with nothing to play for. The Parkhead club could certainly rely on superior experience. The XI likely to take the field against St Mirren could boast 20 league winners medals between them to Hearts' three, all of which belonged to Sandy Jardine. With five honours since the turn of the decade Celtic, whatever their current travails, certainly had the edge in terms of performing on the big occasion.

Three years on and Celtic were once more hoping Dundee would do them a favour to save them from last-gasp heartbreak. If the impossible was to become possible then St Mirren had to be slaughtered first and foremost. Only then could they turn their attention to events at Dens Park.

Thursday, 1st May 1986

As MacDonald and Jardine attempted to protect their players from the media glare around Tynecastle with only two days of the league season left they had a lot to thank their old club – and its new manager, in particular – for.

Rangers had endured one of the most serious crises in their 114-year history. The club hadn't won the league for eight years and had secured only a solitary Scottish Cup triumph since the turn of the decade. The side had failed to mount a serious title challenge for years and European qualification was by no means a foregone conclusion, never mind Rangers competing with the giants of the continent. Serious questions were now being asked about the direction the club was moving in. Manager Jock Wallace had broken Celtic's record-breaking run of nine successive league titles and led Rangers to two domestic trebles in his first spell in the hot seat but when he returned to Ibrox in 1983 he had been unable to prevent the slide that had begun under John Greig. In the three seasons that followed Wallace enjoyed a win ratio of less than 50 per cent and discontent amongst supporters was evident as crowds at Ibrox dipped below five-figures on several occasions.

The semi-final disappointment at Hibs' hands was as close as Rangers got to glory in 85/86. The club's UEFA Cup campaign ended with a first round defeat to Spanish side Osasuna and the Gers also fell at the first hurdle in the Scottish as Hearts run to the final began. The league season had begun promisingly with Rangers winning five and drawing one of their opening half-dozen matches only for the club to enter into a period of prolonged inconsistency just as Hearts' star was on the rise. Going into the final game of the season, a visit from second-bottom Motherwell, the Ibrox men needed to win to limp into Europe the following season. Having lost 14 games and won only 12 up to that point, two points were far from a formality and Rangers were already destined to finish the season with fewer points than games played for the first time in their history.

For an institution of Rangers' size, the situation was intolerable and the board had already made the shock announcement that club legend Wallace was to be replaced by Rangers' first player/manager, the legendary midfield hardman Graeme Souness. Fifty-four-times capped Scottish international Souness had been a key part of the all-conquering Liverpool team of the late 1970s and early 1980s before heading for pastures new and a successful spell with Italian club Sampdoria. The Genoa side were willing to let Souness return to his homeland for £300,000, but only on the condition he saw out his final Serie A season first. Coach Alex Totten took temporary charge of the Ibrox side while Walter Smith, who was to be Souness' assistant negotiated his release from Dundee United. Smith filled the hot seat while waiting for his gaffer to arrive but there was no upturn in fortunes as three successive away matches saw Rangers pick up a single point as Dundee eliminated the gap between the two mid-table sides.

Wallace's fate had been sealed towards the end of March after Rangers' dramatic 4-4 draw with Celtic at Ibrox. Celtic played for almost an hour with 10 men after Willie McStay was sent off as his team led 2-0. Rangers pulled one back before their shorthanded opponents made it 3-1 but their numerical superiority seemed to be telling when they scored three goals in 11 minutes. Rather than seeing out the game at 4-3, Rangers allowed their lead to slip and were unable to regain it after Celtic equalised with 20 minutes to go. Under the circumstances it appeared to be a point dropped by the hosts and the new Rangers managing director David Holmes was dismayed by the scenes of celebration orchestrated by the manager and others at the club. For Rangers men such as Wallace, causing Celtic to fall further behind leaders Hearts and second-place Dundee United after a game they were widely expected to win represented a victory of sorts.

For Holmes and Lawrence Marlborough, the Nevada-based businessman who had recently acquired control of the club, simply hoping Celtic dealt with upstarts from the east as badly as the Light Blues wasn't enough. They had staked their reputations and money on ensuring Rangers once again became the pre-eminent force in Scottish football and the support were behind their new owners in their quest. First though, there was the conclusion of this season to deal with and Souness was to take charge of his first match against Motherwell.

"It had been a terrible season and a terrible few years," recalled Rangers supporter Hamish Strachan. "There were players on the park who honestly seemed to serve any purpose – there were players at the club who were average at best. That was reflected in the crowds we were getting. When Jock Wallace came back we thought he'd send players into games

55

with battle fever but he just wasn't the same manager, the club wasn't the same and the other teams in the league – with Aberdeen, United and now Hearts being strong – weren't the same either. The team was weak and bullied in a lot of games. He was brought back in the hope he could produce his previous managerial performances but it just didn't happen with the current squad of players.

"We were getting excited and looking to the future since it was announced Souness would be taking over. What we thought was that he would have player power, in that his reputation and personality would appeal to a far higher standard of player than we were otherwise able to attract at the time. Saying 'come to Rangers and maybe finish 5th in the Premier League' wasn't much of a sell but suddenly we were thinking that as long as the board could find the money to back him then we knew we would be a much more attractive proposition. As much as anything, we were also getting a great player and one who would certainly bring a lot of dig to the team and that was something we were badly lacking."

Having played his last game for Sampdoria the same weekend as Hearts were scraping past Clydebank and an unimpressive Celtic were beating Dundee, Souness arrived at Ibrox to meet his new charges a few days later. The visit of Motherwell would mark his managerial debut and the excitement surrounding his arrival ensured a media frenzy when he held his inaugural press conference as Rangers manager on the first day of May. However romantic the Hearts story was, the fourth estate could not resist the return of one of Scotland's greatest ever players. The prodigal son was a highly decorated enforcer who had proven himself on the world stage but whose talents had never graced the domestic game in Scotland. And he was coming to save a footballing empire from collapse. The Ibrox giants were certainly keen to capitalise on the excitement of Souness's arrival and announced on the day of his press conference that season tickets – priced from £50 and £30 for the Enclosure to £250 in the Ibrox Suite – would be going on sale two weeks early this year and would be available to buy when Rangers hosted Motherwell on Saturday.

Souness had met Marlbrough before facing a press pack desperate to know what their chat meant in terms of recruitment. Souness said he had made contact with three big names, all of whom "are desperate to come to Ibrox" and wanted them under contract before he left for Mexico as part of the Scottish World Cup squad in a fortnight. He admitted one was his international team-mate Richard Gough, although Dundee United had already turned down a £500,000 bid from Rangers, and another was currently plying his trade abroad. That led *Glasgow Herald* reporter Ian Paul to speculate that it may be England star Trevor Francis, who Souness had played alongside at Sampdoria. Paul added that if it were Francis, "the implications are manifold in that he is apparently a Catholic – isn't it a nonsense that this has to be part of the report?"

The fact that a European Cup winner, England's first £1million player, joining the ranks at Ibrox would have implications other than footballing ones spoke volumes about the times and Rangers lingering sectarian signing policy. Souness had already made it plain that he would sign a Catholic player if he felt they would make Rangers stronger on the pitch, leading to excited ruminations about who that footballer might be.

"Alex Ferguson and Jim McLean had both been approached about taking the Rangers job and although both were told they could sign players of any religious persuasion they still turned down the overtures from Ibrox," said football writer Ron Scott. "So the club's position had changed by the time Souness arrived because he made it clear from the very outset he would sign who he wanted regardless of religion or anything else other than footballing ability."

Earlier in the week, Ian Paul's paper had carried a report claiming that a free transfer from Tottenham could become Souness's first Catholic signing. "21-year-old Dick, from Stirling, is an ex-pupil of St Modens High School," it said, "Dick's father, David, is a Protestant and his mother, Mary, is a Catholic." The Scottish media was rarely as inquisitive as when it came to investigating the religious affiliations of Rangers transfer targets. In Scottish football there existed a seemingly inexhaustible supply of informants passing on details of a player or referee's background to confirm the prejudices of the masses. It was in this atmosphere of suspicion and paranoia that fans began to reflect on the motivations of Hearts and Celtic's last-day opponents.

"I have never known any professional footballer who went on the park wanting anything other than to win and who doesn't try, regardless of who they are playing," said then St Mirren captain Tony Fitzpatrick. "People heard about the background of this player or that and thought 'he'll be at it'. It's sad that the fact my name is Fitzpatrick rather than Wilson or whatever else means I must have supported a team and people feel entitled to doubt your professionalism and commitment but that's Scottish football for you though. I wasn't conflicted in any way that game. The more high-profile your opponent the more you want to beat them. I was representing St Mirren and that's all there was to it. Our build up was the same as it ever was. Our manager was as thorough as he ever was. We worked all week to a specific plan how we could take both points."

The Love Street club sat two points behind both Rangers and Dundee but season-long defensive problems equated to the third-worst goal difference in the league and no prospect of European qualification regardless of what happened at Ibrox and Dens.

Amongst Buddies fans there was a feeling of frustration that the club's golden period was passing without tangible success save for becoming the first and only team north of the border to win the Anglo-Scottish Cup. It was at Paisley that Alex Ferguson first made his mark as a manager, joining the club in 1974 after just six months at East Stirlingshire, his first spell in the dugout. Ferguson took over the reigns at Love Street aged just 32 and utterly transformed the club, taking them from the bottom half of the old Division Two and playing in front of only around 1000 to packed houses as they secured their Premier Division safety three-and-a-half years later.

Despite this, Ferguson would be sacked by St Mirren (the only club to do so in his illustrious career) under controversial circumstances. Chairman Willie Todd would claim Ferguson had "no managerial ability" at a subsequent employment tribunal that ruled against the disposed manager but his legacy was the basis for one of the most successful periods in the club's history. Ferguson discovered and blooded youngsters like Fitzpatrick, Billy Stark, Lex Richardson, Frank McGarvey, Bobby Reid and Peter Weir while turning St Mirren into a dynamic attacking side and successors Jim Clunie and Rikki McFarlane benefited from the foundations laid by Fergie. In addition to their Anglo-Scottish success, the Buddies also finished third in the Premier Division, their highest ever league position, in 1980 and a further two European campaigns followed while the club regularly reached the latter stages of cup competitions in the first part of the decade.

Now led by the pragmatic Alex Miller, the St Mirren side that had served Ferguson, Clunie and McFarlane so well had now departed and a new clutch of young players, including Brian Hamilton and Steve Clarke, were breaking through. Transitional period or not, a seventh place finish was disappointing by St Mirren's recent standards and most people involved with the club would rather the season had already ended.

Lifelong Buddie David MacDonald remembered, "Growing up I saw probably the greatest ever St Mirren team, one that regularly got to semi-finals, and we even came close to winning the league one year. We finished third but were right in the mix until the end of the season. In 85-86 there was a bit of a break up of the great side but we were still a well established, mid-table team that got into Europe on occasion and were a good team.

"I was going to the game at Love Street hoping Hearts would win the league. There were loads of Rangers and Celtic fans at school and in the streets and I never wanted them to win. The whole week I was thinking that we'd get a good laugh at their plight because I didn't think there was any way they would win the league."

MacDonald wasn't the only non-Celtic fan to have ruled them out of the running. Fired up by Souness's arrival and the impending changes at Ibrox, Hamish Strachan remembers being relaxed about the season's climax. "In the run up I didn't give it too much thought because I thought Hearts would do it," he said. "They only had to get a draw and I thought they'd get the result they needed. I thought Celtic would get the goals they needed and maybe put pressure on Hearts but they would do the business themselves."

On the back of their astonishing run, avoiding defeat at Dens appeared well within Hearts' capabilities and, even allowing for a slip-up, a four-goal swing was needed to prevent the title heading to Gorgie. A single-goal victory for Dundee would be meaningless unless Celtic won by three or more. If Dundee were to win by two clear goals, Celtic would have to at least match the achievement at Paisley. In the unlikely event of Dundee winning by three or more goals any Celtic victory would do. As Celtic supporters woke up the morning after the Motherwell game they knew their mission remained, if not impossible, highly improbable. This was Hearts' story, this was their song. Hundreds of thousands of Hoops fans across the world looked on impotently knowing there was nothing they could do to influence events.

There was, however, one Celtic supporter about to enter the stage and prove his virility in a style as spectacular as it was unlikely.

Friday, 2nd May 1986

The discussion taking place in the Tynecastle manager's office was an unwelcome one. Despite attempts at containment, two more first-team squad members – Brian Whittaker and George Cowie – had been laid low by the flu bug and MacDonald and Jardine were forced to consider contingency plans ahead of their date with destiny.

Sixty miles to the north the manager's office at Dens Park was also about to become the location for a conference that would have far-reaching consequences. Dundee boss Archie Knox worked on preparations for the following day's match at his desk, unaware that one of his less favoured players was at that moment standing on the other side of the door, working up the courage to plead for the opportunity to play a part in the club's final push for a European spot. He stood little over 5'7 tall and sported thick black curls and a moustache that saw him likened to comic Bobby Ball. His name was Albert Kidd.

Hearts didn't have the luxury of last-day opponents with nothing to play for. Knox's improving Dundee side were still locked in a battle for European qualification with Rangers; the Light Blues and Dark Blues tied on 33 points. Rangers needed full points on the final day to be sure of the final slot in next season's UEFA Cup as Dundee would pip them at the line if they could better their result when they hosted the champions-elect. A vastly superior goal difference and the strength of the Dark Blues' opponents were the main factors in the Gers' favour as the big day approached.

"I wasn't caring about who won the title," remembered Dundee supporter Barry Davidson. "We were going for Europe and had our own job to do so couldn't think about Hearts, Celtic or anyone else. No one gave us a chance but that never particularly annoyed me. Hearts had gone so long without defeat you understood why everyone thought they'd get the draw at least. Probably deep down we felt we were just going to come up short as well."

Although the prize at stake for Dundee players and fans fell short of the riches awaiting everyone associated with Heart of Midlothian, no one should have underestimated the desire of the Dens Park side to see their name in the draw for the following season's UEFA Cup. League winners and semi-finalists in both the European Cup and Fairs Cup in the 1960s, Dundee's fall from grace had been even more spectacular than Hearts'.

The club was relegated in the first year of the new Premier Division and consigned to a financially ruinous three years outside the top flight. They then bounced between the two leagues before finally establishing some kind of stability under first Donald MacKay and then Knox. That first relegation had come as a complete shock as the Dark Blues had gone the previous six seasons without finishing outside the top six, but it was only confirmed after city rivals United beat Rangers in a rearranged match after the Ibrox side had secured the treble and decided to rest several key players. Dundee finished the season level on points with Aberdeen and United, who went on to thrive in the new set up, but went down on goal difference.

Not having played competitive football on the continent since 1974/75, Europe was an obsession bordering on the 'Faragian' for Dundee and its fans in the 1980s. The Dark Blues prodigious youth system unearthed players of the quality of Gordon Strachan, Stewart McKimmie, Iain Ferguson and Ian Redford only for the need to sell to survive to frustrate successive managers' team-building efforts. Europe was seen as the panacea to Dundee's ills – it would steady the club's finances, prevent talented youngsters leaving, attract a better quality of signing and be the first step towards closing the sizable gap that United had opened up over the past decade. In a city at the forefront of the UK's embryonic computer games industry, one group of tech entrepreneurs had even released a football management simulation – *Dundee's European Challenge* – inspired by the ambition.

Davidson continued, "Donald MacKay's team was okay then when Archie came in we really stepped up and looked a decent side, with signings like Jim Duffy, Stuart Rafferty, Bobby Connor and John Brown. I think in any other era we would have been classed as a really good team but it clashed with Aberdeen and United having the best periods in their whole history, Celtic being strong and then a resurgent Hearts. It was pretty mental as I don't remember Hearts looking anything special the previous year when we beat them three times and drew the other. Like I said we were no mugs ourselves and usually around the fringes of Euro qualification and I probably considered Hearts similar. To step up like that when everything seemed to click for them was quite surreal."

Knox had been Alex Ferguson's assistant at Aberdeen and was in the dugout the night of the Pittodrie club's greatest achievement – beating the mighty Real Madrid in the 1983 European Cup-Winners' Cup final in Gothenburg. Shortly afterwards he accepted the offer to replace Donald MacKay, who had resigned as Dundee manager after becoming frustrated with the board's decision to sell his star players, and, over the next three seasons he was to turn Dundee from perennial strugglers to a comfortable mid-table side on the verge of realising their European desires while at the same time improving their horrendous cup and derby records.

Hardly blessed with inexhaustible reserves of cash, Knox proved himself to be a shrewd operator in the transfer market as he scoured the dregs of the Premier Division and lower leagues for bargain buys with the ability to step up. Connor, Brown, Rafferty and others flourished under Knox's guidance and, allied to youngsters such as Tosh McKinlay and Rab Shannon and marquee signing Jim Duffy, the foundations of a more than decent team had been assembled at Dens Park. The Dark Blues were still troubled by inconsistency and a lack of strength in depth but, on their day, Knox's Dundee team were a match for most.

One name that would be missing from the list of Dundee's top players compiled by any Dundee fan that season was that of Albert Kidd. The Dundonian had become the Dark Blues' record signing after his performances at Motherwell, where he averaged better than a goal every three games from midfield, persuaded Donald MacKay to shell out £80,000 for his services in 1981. Kidd struggled to recapture the form he had shown at Fir Park and, as of the 2nd May 1986 had managed to score a modest 10 times in his 114 league appearances for Dundee. Frustrated at what they saw as a big-money flop, fans failed to take to Kidd and the player himself freely admits that he struggled to make his mark at Dens.

"Ally MacLeod and Davie Hay were my managers at Motherwell and they were great with me, they really knew how to push my buttons," he explained. "I felt comfortable there and scored goals but Motherwell were in the First Division and the chance to move to the Premier was a big ticket item for me," he explained. "I was driving every day down to Motherwell from Dundee. It was a total headache so I was allowed to train at Tannadice a couple of days a week. We had drawn United in a two-legged cup tie, and I played really well. I was a real thorn in their side. Wee Jim was not daft. I was training at Dundee United and he probably allowed that to have a look at me. My dad was a Dundee fan, my wife's family is totally Dundee. So it would have been a bit of a headache for the family if I signed for United.

"It was great to sign for Dundee but I felt a lot of pressure. It was my hometown and everyone knew me and my family and I've joined for a lot of money. I felt it immediately. When I signed Donald told me that he wanted to build the team around me. It never happened. I never really thought Dundee used me in my best position, which in my opinion is in the middle of midfield in an attacking sense. I always played wide or upfront in a wide position.

"Being a Dundee boy, feeling the pressure of expectations and not being used as I'd expected, I lost confidence. It was a difficult time for me. My confidence was at an all time low and looking back now, I understand how any footballer can in many ways look an ordinary player when they lose that confidence. I had a back injury plus I needed an operation after breaking my nose and not being able to breathe correctly. New players came in and we had a better team so it became more difficult to bed down a position."

When MacKay resigned and Archie Knox was appointed as his replacement, Kidd initially felt it gave his faltering Dens Park career a boost.

"I was pleased when Archie was appointed. He used to coach me when I played boys' football and I really liked Archie. I just don't think he did me any favours. With today's modern techniques in sports science you can measure lactic acid tolerance etc. but how that was explained in the old days was whether someone had a good engine on them or not. To be honest with you, I never had a good engine. I was never a player who could run up and down the park all day. But if you got me in the final third, I could always beat a player and put a good cross in or beat a player and have a shot. I had good vision and was two-footed, and I just felt I was never used in that capacity. I was always played in a wide midfield position and was expected to get up and down the park. That wasn't me. By the time I got into a good position my legs didn't have it in them to do anything."

Ron Scott, who watched Kidd's career develop from its early days, agrees that he and Knox were far from a perfect fit.

"Albert had only started four league games that season and had only scored against Hamilton in the League Cup. He was an old-fashioned ball-carrying player. He loved to run with the ball. He signed for a lot of money in those days, which puts pressure on you right away. He did okay under Donald MacKay but Archie wanted him to cover every blade of grass and that wasn't Albert's game. He could get forward with the ball no problem but couldn't get up and down the park all day like Archie wanted him to do."

"There was one time I questioned Archie," Kidd remembers. "People's heads were full of so much tactics that they had forgotten about the most important thing – putting the ball in the back of the net. I used to come down the line and think, 'I can't check inside here because I've been told if I check inside again I'm coming off.' It was the standard way of treating players then though. Fergie and Wee Jim had the same harsh style. I remember playing Aberdeen at Dens one afternoon and the noise coming out of the dressing room was alarming. The obscenities. And I witnessed that right across the board. It wasn't the done thing to be positive and encouraging. That only happened if we won. If you were having a bad spell, out of favour, not in the plans, it was a dreadful environment.

"My teammate Bobby Glennie always said to me, 'You're one of the best players in this team, I cannot believe the manager is not playing you'. I am not saying I was Ronaldo but I know I had more to offer and that if I had been managed better I could have had a better career. I always thought I should have been in the 11 or 13 at least. I used to blitz it in training because I was more relaxed then. A few of the boys were like, 'Ach, you are just a training player'. They were having a bit of fun but I still maintain I was never used properly.

"I remember playing against Richard Gough and giving him an absolute bath at Dens. But it was always in the final third. When I needed to get back down the park, well that wasn't my role, or it shouldn't have been. I think Archie liked me but I just felt he never used me right. He played me in role I didn't have the capacity for.

"When we went away for pre-season, I was always the top scorer or one of the top scorers. But when we got back to Scotland it never really happened for me. I had always fancied playing abroad and always seemed to do well overseas. I played well against teams like Borussia Dortmund, Bayer Leverkusen, Eintracht Frankfurt etc. I really enjoyed the freedom of playing in what was a less tight environment than Scotland. Archie had an offer for me from Fortuna Dusseldorf on the back of my performances in Germany but it fell through for some reason. I never did hear what actually happened."

If his manager was hardly over-enamoured with the misfiring forward he had inherited from his predecessor, the relationship between Kidd and Knox's assistant Jocky Scott was more antagonistic. Kidd earned £110 a week but his chances to top up his wage with appearance money and bonuses for goals scored were by this point limited. So far that season he had made only 11 appearances, seven of which were as a substitute, as Harvey, Ray Stephen, Ross Jack and future Scotland captain Colin Hendry, then a striker, were placed ahead of Kidd in the pecking order. And yet here he was, on the eve of Scotland's biggest game of the season, perhaps even several years given the interest in the Hearts' fairytale, knocking on the gaffer's door to plead for the chance to show what he could do. The suspension that Stephen, the club's top marksman with 18 goals that term, picked up as a result of his red card at Parkhead ruled him out of the final game of the season. This was good news for both Hearts and one of Dundee's out-of-favour forwards. 'Why shouldn't it be me?' Kidd asked himself as he took a deep breath and knocked on the manager's door.

"The season was a write off for me," admitted Kidd. "I wasn't happy at that time. My confidence was not good. If you are not playing, you are not happy. I picked up injuries, that didn't help. I was certainly on the outside, playing a lot of reserve football. And I was still pretty young at the time.

"I wasn't in the squad. It was the last game of the season so I thought I'd chance it and remind the manager that I had a pretty decent record throughout my career against Hearts. It was the Friday around 11 o'clock in the morning. I had trained well and had been finishing well all week. I was capable of scoring goals, no doubt. I thought I had nothing to lose. You have to push your own barrow.

"I said to him, 'Look, I'd just like to say you should consider me for tomorrow, I have a really good track record against Hearts'. He says, 'What do you mean?' I said, 'Whenever I have played against Hearts, I have done well for some unknown reason. I am not trying to force your hand. I am just saying if you look at my history, I have always done well against them, even when I was at Arbroath and Motherwell.'

"He said, 'Okay, I will consider it. Appreciate you coming in'. I never thought any more about it. I thought it would just fall on deaf ears. The team had been picked. I went home and Archie's secretary, Bronwyn, called me to say I was in the squad for tomorrow."

It was a shock for Kidd, who, with only a year left on his contract, knew he was running out of time to make an impression at his home town club. He had grown up in the newly built Charleston housing scheme. In its early days, Charleston largely served an overspill development for neighbouring Lochee, the area of Dundee that had become home to thousands of Irish immigrants seeking work in the jute industry. Dundee United's David Narey grew up a few streets from Kidd and his Dundee teammate Bobby Glennie lived a short distance away. Firebrand politician George Galloway and 'the Bard of Dundee' Michael Marra were others who grew up in the Lochee/Charleston area in the 1950s and 60s.

Like many of his contemporaries in the area and at St Clement's Primary and St John's High School, Kidd followed Celtic as a youngster. While many of his schoolmates could date their family's support for the Parkhead giants back generations, Kidd's father was actually a Dundee fan. It was watching the all-conquering Lisbon Lions become the first British club to win the European Cup that seduced a young Albert.

"I remember watching the European Cup final in 1967 and can still reel off the team now," he said. "My older brother was pretty Celtic-orientated and I remember getting the tracksuit and collecting their programmes. My father took me to a final when I was young. I never took any interest in any other club."

By his teens, Kidd was establishing a reputation for himself as a young footballer of considerable potential and he spent four summers training with Arsenal alongside other promising Scottish youths. The Highbury club were to take their interest no further and Kidd signed for Brechin City. A successful spell on loan at Carnoustie Panmure juniors led to Dundee United manager Jim McLean putting in a bid for Kidd, only for his father to insist the 16-year-old turn them down and complete an apprenticeship as a toolmaker. The interest led to Kidd being recalled by his parent club and within a year he had signed for fellow Angus club Arbroath for £10,000. Kidd was made Arbroath captain at the age of 20 and again attracted the interest of Jim McLean but eventually chose to sign for Ally MacLeod's Motherwell instead. Jock Wallace, then manager of Leicester City, also had Kidd down for a trial before he left to retake the hotseat at Ibrox. Two seasons at Motherwell saw Kidd maintain a decent scoring record from an attacking midfield berth and United attempted to sign him for a third time, offering the Fir Park club Derek Addison and Graeme Payne in exchange. City rivals Dundee offered Motherwell hard cash, however, and the money on offer proved more appealing to a club then struggling to gain promotion to the Premier Division.

Whatever his feelings about how he was used at Dens Park by Donald MacKay, Archie Knox and Jocky Scott, who served as number two to both managers, Kidd admits that he could perhaps have adopted a more professional approach at times.

"I used to go and shoot geese before training," he laughed. "Me and George McGeachie were big shooters. I remember bringing wild geese into Dens in the morning and the boys were in the bath getting their legs warmed up. I would throw a couple wild geese in with them! I remember meeting Donald MacKay at the front door and I had all the green stuff on, the camouflage etc. He was like, 'Where the fuck have you been?' I said, 'Oh, just doing a bit of shooting this morning, for an hour or so'. In actual fact we'd been there at 4.30am – then going training. Pretty bad attitude but there you go.

"There was a laddish element then. I was not a ring-leader but I was up for a laugh. I remember a pre-season tour of North America. Tosh McKinlay was very young at the time, and had a pair of leather trousers. We went to a nightclub. This was the night before the game and the curfew was 11pm. There was a 'best ass' competition – we put young Tosh up and he won!

"Me, Bobby Glennie, Cammy Fraser, 'Cowboy' McCormack and Ray Stephen were left - it was 12 o'clock. Cowboy is at the bar and he is puffing on this cigar, saying, 'This is fantastic.' I'm going 'Yes, it's good but we better get moving.' We get back to the hotel and Cowboy opens the taxi door and he just collapses onto the pavement, physically falls out of the car. Archie is coming down the stairs – 'What the fuck have you been doing?' I tried to claim we'd only had three pints of lager but Cowboy takes the moment to start laying into him. 'Look at him, the big manager, up on his pedestal.' Archie said, 'That's it! The two of you are going home tomorrow.' There was about two weeks of the tour left.

The next morning I went to the manager's room and apologised. He said, 'Okay wee man. You are in the squad again, but you are not playing tonight.' Archie put us on the bench for some reason. The humidity was incredible. I was sitting next to Cowboy watching the guys running about sweating and we were thinking we'd had a lucky escape. We were out at half-time, strutting around, hung over. Our physio Eric Ferguson comes out – 'Albert! Cowboy!' We came back to the dressing room and Archie said to me, 'Play up front on the right. Cowboy, play right side of midfield. And if I see the two of you walking once in the whole second half, no spending money for the rest of the tour.' From sitting having a laugh on the bench we came off the park absolutely knackered. But we won 2-1."

With the majority of Dundee's players hailing from the west coast, and with one of the Old Firm still competing for the league title, the situation at the top of the table was proving a distraction to the squad as they prepared for Hearts' visit, as Kidd explained. "There were Rangers fans like 'Bomber' Brown and others in the dressing room but also Celtic supporters like Tosh, Duff, Cowboy, me and Lexie so there was a fair bit of banter about who was going to win the league but the priority was us. The aim for all of us was to get Dundee into Europe. Of course, if Celtic benefited from that then I wasn't going to be unhappy. We lived in the shadow of a good Dundee United team so it was vital for us. We were really close as a group and had a good, happy dressing room. We spent a lot of time away together on pre-season tours. We were desperate to experience proper European football together as a team."

Ironically, the situation Dundee found themselves in was remarkably similar to the season before when, once again, Hearts were among the main players in the drama. On that occasion, Dundee went into the final game a point behind fifth-place St Mirren in the race for the final UEFA Cup spot and needed the Jambos to do them a favour when they visited Love Street. Things could hardly have gone worse for Hearts, and by extension the Dark Blues, as the Buddies romped to a 5-2 victory. The last two goals were conceded by Sandy Jardine after Henry Smith was injured as substitute goalkeepers remained a far-off luxury. Whilst the trauma of that day fell short of the despair Dundee fans felt watching their main rivals celebrate on their patch in 1983, they were once again fated to endure last-day taunts as they missed out on Europe despite beating United 1-0. The Terrors losing the Scottish Cup final to Celtic the following week would at least provide some respite for the long-suffering Dees.

"Derbies are all about bragging rights so winning one was never painful," said Davidson. "Celtic beating United in the final the next week meant it wasn't a bad end to the year, although it was obviously disappointing to miss out on Europe after a few bad results towards the end of the season."

Yet again Dundee required a club with nothing to play for to rise to the occasion and yet again they were left with no room for error themselves. This time around, though, they were coming up against a side with more than local bragging rights to play for and they needed big performances from big players and for their wily manager to get everything right in his preparation and on the day. How would their fans have felt on the eve of the game to know that Albert Kidd was set to come in from the cold ahead of more obvious candidates for a place in the squad?

"I think for most people, he was regarded as average and a fringe-type player who had turned it on on a few occasions but had probably disappointed overall," continued Davidson. "He wasn't quite a target for the boo boys but wasn't likely to be mobbed by adoring fans either. Like I said, he was on the fringes so there wouldn't have been anything particularly remarkable about him being involved. His time at Dundee was pretty unremarkable up to that point."

Saturday, 3rd May 1986

"Hearts have finally arrived at their day of reckoning after a journey which began 27 league matches ago," wrote James Traynor in that morning's *Glasgow Herald*. "One more victory and everyone will have to accept what the Tynecastle faithful have been telling us for months. Hearts will be champions." Traynor sounded a note of caution given Dundee's motivation but added that "Hearts have met challenge after challenge with a steely resolve this season and they surely will be crowned around 4.40 this afternoon."

And as for how the Hearts players would deal with the pressure of the occasion? "The fans are probably feeling it more than the players," said Sandy Jardine. "Pressure for us was three years ago when if we did not get promotion we would have been forced to go part-time." Scotland's Footballer of the Year added that his side would play their normal game as to try and do anything else would be foolish.

Celtic manager Davie Hay remained confident that his team would keep up their side of the bargain. "Scoring the necessary amount of goals is not beyond us," he said. "We know, of course, that St Mirren are not going to sit back and let us score, but if we display the same attitude and form of recent weeks it should be enough."

Traynor's preview of the day's action concluded by reminding his readers that the matches at Dens Park and Love Street were not the only shows in town.

Turning to Rangers' situation, he noted that Graeme Souness had been reassured by the club's board that money would be made available to him to substantially strengthen his squad, regardless of whether or not the Ibrox team marked his first game as manager by qualifying for Europe.

The *Herald* piece was one of many that angered Souness's opposite number at Celtic Park that morning. "I had watched a sports programme on TV the night before and I was left with the impression that the silverware was as good as already in the Hearts trophy cabinet," said Hay in the book *Caesar & The Assassin*. "Celtic were being written off by just about everyone. Believe me, that can raise the hackles. The following morning I picked up all the daily newspapers. Sure enough, they followed the same route. It appeared we were wasting our time bothering to fulfil our remaining fixture, the trophy was already bedecked in maroon colours. Oh, really?"

The Saturday press was also a cause of consternation for Hearts fan Mike Smith as the longest week of his life drew to an end at last. "I was travelling down from Aberdeen for the game with my mate and we'd made plans to go to Perth afterwards and meet up with a Jambo pal who lived there to celebrate. I woke up that morning feeling nervous and excited, and still confident. Then I read a copy of the *Daily Record* on the way to Dundee about the events of 1965. It was part of Hearts folklore so, of course I knew about it, but in all the excitement, I hadn't thought about it. Now the first seeds of doubt were planted in my head. I wondered if the same was happening to the Hearts players."

The most offensive Hearts-related coverage in that week's press was surely the puff piece in which Edinburgh-born comedian Ronnie Corbett declared his support for Hearts' title bid by posing in the club's colours. As Corbett stood at little more than five feet tall, finding a Hearts kit to fit him was problematic for the organisers of the photo shoot and, as he struck a light-hearted, high-kicking pose the shorts, surely intended for a child, rode up to inflict Ronnie's underpants on an unsuspecting public.

Hearts' fabulous unbeaten run had given rise to another questionable contribution to the nation's cultural canon. Seeking to capitalise on the feelgood factor surrounding the Tynecastle side a decision was made to record a new version of the club's anthem, famous for its 'Hearts, Hearts, Glorious Hearts' chorus. Officially credited to the Hearts Squad featuring Colin Chisholm, the cover version was a pale imitation of the Hector Nicol original but it was the single's B-side that really plumbed new depths. Commentator Archie MacPherson recited the names of the team and provided a voice-over of match highlights, while a jingle for sponsors Marshall's Chunky Chicken could be heard in the background. The line 'Marshall's, the Chunky Chicken champions' drew comment from many who felt the use of the third c-word was somewhat premature given Hearts had won nothing yet. Tempting providence was the least of John Colquhoun's worries, however. "To be involved in that, for somebody who was a Joy Division fan," he said, "was too embarrassing for words."

If fans were looking to the sky for signs of portentousness, then the outlook was significantly worse for Celtic. Across most of the west coast, rain fell steadily from daybreak while the east was merely gloomy and overcast. Of greater concern to Alex MacDonald was the telephone call he received from a mainstay of his team. Craig Levein had now fallen victim to the flu bug that had afflicted his teammates throughout the week and was too ill to travel to Dundee, let alone play any part in proceedings.

"This was serious, even if Sandy Jardine and I weren't inclined to admit as much publicly," he said in *Doddie*. "We kept our worst fears to ourselves, not least for the reason our many years in football had taught us that excuses count for nothing. Only results matter." Celtic also suffered a late call off when striker Alan McInally was declared unfit to play due to illness, but the loss of one of Scotland's most outstanding young players would surely be more keenly felt by Hearts.

Rumours about the flu bug were by now starting to spread amongst Hearts fans but, as they began congregating for their journeys north, most Jambos remained blissfully unaware of their side's plight. Many Edinburgh pubs played fast and loose with licensing laws to open their doors early to thirsty, maroon-clad fans eager for their first drink of the day to ease nerves and hopefully mark the start of the party to end all parties.

"Our local was running a bus," remembered Bobby Mitchell. "It was a case of making sure no one was watching and knocking on the side door to get let in. I got there about 10 and there were punters who'd obviously been there a while already or who hadn't really stopped from the Friday night."

While the vast majority of the 10,000-plus Jambo

contingent left by car, train and bus from the same city, followers of Celtic, with their massive support spread far across Scotland and beyond began the journey to Love Street from the four corners of the land.

Paul Larkin was among the Celtic fans for whom every fixture was an away day. He lived in Edinburgh and the week leading up to the game had been made more torturous by the prevalence of so many followers of the team even he believed was more likely to become champions by the end of the afternoon.

"Hearts hadn't lost a game since the 28th of September 1985," he said. "Although we had won the last seven games on the bounce, none of them were that convincing. Still, it was the last day of the season, the last chance to see the team in three months. There was also defiance. Being surrounded by Jambos, you felt like you had to hold your head up and keep up a front of confidence."

For those based in Dundee and Paisley, that day's commute was much shorter, if no less tense. Just as Jambos were loading up their carry-outs and hanging maroon scarves from car windows, and as Celtic fans were hitting the motorways, a-roads and side streets that would lead them to Love Street, Albert Kidd was sitting down to his breakfast, wondering if his appeal to Archie Knox would be successful and he would be allowed his chance to shine. He still doubted it.

Back in Edinburgh it was hard for Hibs to avoid the spectacle of their neighbours vacating the city in party mood. Everywhere they looked was the spectacle of Jambos heading towards the station or pub and the chariot that would lead them to the Promised Land. They waited on street corners for their lift, noisily greeting others decked in maroon that passed them. Cars that spotted fellow Jambos honked their horn in recognition, Hearts songs and even renditions of *Championees* could be heard from those whose confidence had been fired by an early start. Being a resident of Leith offered Hibee John Craig some protection, however.

"I managed to avoid it pretty much on the day," he said. "I had got married the year before and our first flat was on Easter Road so I was in pretty much as safe territory as was possible. They were going to win the league, there was no doubt about it, so I just tried to do what I would normally do and not let it affect me too much."

Hoops fan Eddie Toner said, "Even though I was still confident that Celtic would win the league and had, by now, fair a fair amount of money on it, there wasn't much expectation of Hearts blowing it among my mates as we got on the bus for Paisley. I vividly remember meeting in the pub and the owner, who was a big Celtic man, said 'you're not going down there looking for a miracle are you?' You've got to live in hope but it has to be said the atmosphere was fairly low-key going down to Paisley."

Steely determination marked the Celtic team's journey to Love Street after their pre-match meeting at the Grosvenor Hotel in Glasgow's Byres Road, according to Murdo MacLeod. "Being written off wasn't something that bothered me, or anyone else, I don't think," he said. "We all knew what we could do, we had a good team. We were football players going for the league title and playing for a club like Celtic – that was all the motivation you needed.

"There might have been a lot of people that thought all Hearts had to do was turn up but that's not how we saw it. We felt Dundee having Europe to play for was a huge thing in our favour. Dundee had a good side and if that game was played at the start of the season then they probably would have been favourites. Going into a game to win a title and thinking 'just don't lose', is not as easy as you think, especially when the side you're playing also has something to play for."

By the early afternoon, the Jambos had begun arriving in Dundee in considerable numbers, thronging bars and starting up impromptu parties in the street. Those hosting their pre-match festivities in pubs at the top of the Hilltown would have been unaware that their opponents for the day were beginning their own preparations just a few hundred feet away and that Archie Knox was about to spring a surprise on his squad.

"I didn't realise until I met up with Derek McWilliams that he was supposed to be playing and that I was now in the squad instead of him," said Albert Kidd. "We went for a pre-match meal at the Dundee Social Club and made our way to the ground. It wasn't until we got to the dressing room that Archie named his team. I wasn't expecting to get on the bench until then and still thought it was unlikely I'd get on."

While the majority of Dark Blues were still to make their way to Dens Park, one young Dundee supporter had already reported for duty. Then a 15-year-old programme seller, Barry Davidson was afforded a ringside seat of Hearts fans' pre-match activities.

"When the Old Firm, United or Aberdeen were

here you made sure you had your patch and got selling early as there were usually fans roaming about
from around noon," he said "That day Hearts were
like the Old Firm on steroids. When I got up to the
ground there were hundreds of punters in maroon
wandering about or sitting on grass across from players' entrance, a mixture of waiting on gates opening
and waiting on team bus. A real party atmosphere
was starting. Guys sitting with their carry-out and
waving flags. The police seemed to be happy to take
a back step and just let them have their day. Everyone
was singing 'We're gonna win the league' and 'We
are the champions'. The 'Glorious Hearts' song was
on repeat.

"Back then the programme was quite a big thing
to be bought. Not only was it a souvenir but you got
club, manager and player news that nowadays you
would read on Twitter days before the match. It was
quite common to sell handfuls to the same punter but
I remember that day guys buying up to 10 at a time
and returning to their cars with them, no doubt for
friends and family who couldn't make it that day.

"From my pitch I had seen quite a few scraps over
the years, particularly as the casual scene grew and
peaked in the 80s. That day though there was nobody
looking for trouble. I think all Jambos came as 'scar-
fers' that day and were out to enjoy it. The only time
you normally saw the 'hats, scarfs and badges' ven-
dors was when Rangers or Celtic were in town but
that day there were guys selling League Champions
flags and they were selling like hot cakes. If there
were any fans scared they'd jinx it by buying them
they were in the minority. I don't remember any
nerves among their fans, why would there be? Their

team had went 27 games without defeat and they had the insurance of Celtic needing to win by a barrow-load. Expectation was probably the main feeling and they were there to enjoy it."

The atmosphere could hardly have been more different back in Edinburgh, where Hibees made their way to their side's meeting with Dundee United under a cloud of doom, as John Craig remembered: "There was a really poor crowd, even allowing for it being the end of the season and us having nothing to play for. No one really wanted to be at Easter Road that day. I think a lot of boys barricaded themselves in or occupied themselves elsewhere so they didn't have to think about football.

"When the season had started a Hearts fan at work was telling me how great they would do and how much we'd struggle. At the time I was just thinking, 'ah, typical Jambo blowhard' but now I was thinking how he'd been right all along. That said, most Hearts supporters couldn't believe it themselves. I went to the pub before the game and walked to the ground with pals just like I always did. The way I saw it I was going to watch Hibs and go home again and that was all I was trying to think about. I avoided watching television and reading newspapers and tried to avoid all the build-up and previews as much as possible.

"There was a funereal atmosphere going to the game but no one was talking about the Hearts situation. It was inevitable and once it happened then we would deal with it. That was our feeling. We weren't looking forward to them coming back and hearing them celebrating but the sooner it was over the better. If we started to hope for a shock then it would have led to more disappointment because the odds were so stacked in their favour that no one thought there was any possibility of a surprise."

Football journalist Ron Scott was another who felt the Celts and Hibees were doomed to disappointment. "I went to Love Street not believing Celtic really had a chance," he said. "It was Hearts' league as far as I, and everyone else, was concerned. Doug Baillie covered the Dundee-Hearts game. He was the Post's chief football writer in those days and I the paper's number two. The fact that I was sent to Paisley while Doug travelled through from Glasgow to Dundee, where I lived, tells you how sure everyone was about who was winning the league. The Dens press box was packed with chief football writers while the rank and file were at Love Street. Every paper wanted their number one writer where the winners were to cover the celebrations."

Celtic boss Hay had decided to use the certainty of the media to motivate his players, as he later explained. "I gave one of the shortest team talks I have ever given any team," he later explained, "I asked one of the backroom staff to cut out all the articles from the newspapers relating to ourselves and Hearts. The cuttings were pinned to the walls in the Love Street dressing room. When we arrived, I simply said to the players, 'Go and read those notices'...I looked around the dressing room and all I could see were determined expressions."

Confidence was also growing amongst the Parkhead side's followers, according to Eddie Toner. "We went to the pub we always went to when visiting Love Street. After a few beers we were feeling more confident and the songs were starting up. We started making our way to the ground and got ourselves to our usual spot on the terraces. There was a big Celtic support and we were all feeding off each other."

For Celtic's opponents, the size of the travelling support meant being massively outnumbered on their own turf. "At the time my dad wouldn't let me go to Rangers and Celtic games but on this occasion me and my pals managed to make something up and went along," said Buddie David MacDonald. "I was hoping we'd get a good laugh at them because I didn't think there was any way they would win the league. For as many of them came along as well I can't imagine many of them thought they would either. They let them in our end, behind both goals and we were pushed up into one small section near the corner of the old North Bank. The whole ground was rammed with Celtic. It happened all the time back then. The club gave them as much as they wanted to try and make a few bob and it wasn't something that ever bothered me as it made for a great atmosphere. You're up by that fence with banter and other things flying overhead and it got a bit crazy whenever there was a goal.

"It wasn't unusual for them to come en masse like that but it seemed they had done so more than ever that day. It was wall-to-wall Celtic in the streets surrounding the ground and there were the usual street sellers. It was green-and-white everywhere."

St Mirren's cause was hardly helped by an injury to goalkeeper Campbell Money minutes before Hay offered his players some choice reading material. "We had to get special permission to replace Campbell in goal after he got injured in the warm-up," said his teammate Tony Fitzpatrick. "It was ten to three before we were given permission to play Jim Stewart. That wasn't ideal preparation for a huge game."

Back at Dens Park, the attention of the home fans was divided between the game about to kick off and the one at Ibrox but the nation's premier football writers and those on the away terraces were focused on one thing only.

"We didn't think it would matter what Celtic did," said Mike Smith. "We were surely going to see it out. I don't remember anyone clamouring round radios. We thought we would do it. One win, one point even, was all we needed without bothering with what was happening at Love Street. There was a carnival atmosphere amongst the Hearts fans when we arrived, well over 10,000 singing and dancing. Then rumours circulated about a sickness virus affecting the Hearts team. We watched the players warm up on the Dens Park pitch – they looked fine to us. Hang on, though – there was no sign of Craig Levein." Levein was the only one of the flu victims not to make the squad for that day, although Kenny Black was deemed to be fit enough for a place on the bench only, while Brian Whittaker started despite being well below par.

One man who was out on the park limbering up at that time was Albert Kidd. "There were a hell of a lot of Hearts supporters, probably more than Dundee supporters," he said. "I remember warming up and getting a bit of stick, not that they probably knew who I was then."

After the players made their way back to the dressing room, Archie Knox reminded of them what they were playing for that day. "His team talk was all about Europe," continued Kidd. "He told us to just forget everything else and go out and win the game. Then we'll see where we are. Not to worry about anything else, Hearts, Rangers...anything."

"Who, way back in August, blessed with the second sight of the seventh son of a seventh son could have foreseen that Hearts, on the very last day of the season would be playing for the championship requiring only one point," was how Archie MacPherson opened his commentary of the Dens Park showdown. "They have brought through to the city something like 10,000 supporters, eager and looking forward to the start of the match. But particularly at the end when they hear the final whistle, they have in their massed ranks the confidence that they'll take the championship back to Edinburgh."

With Hearts supporters crammed into the terraces behind the goal to the east of the ground and underneath the ancient, cranked grandstand, the rendition of 'Hello, hello, we are the Gorgie boys' that greeted the away team as they emerged from the tunnel was audible as far south as the city centre. Jambos clambered up the fence at the back of the TC Keay end and swung their legs over the perimeter wall that separated terrace from track, both to obtain a better view of proceedings and to obtain respite from the crush. Gaps could be seen at the far end of the ground but not so much as a square foot of space was available on any of the other three sides. The Hearts end was a sea of maroon as scarves were raised and flags – some emblazoned with 'Champions' – waved and the fans swayed to and fro, heady with anticipation. The Dundee supporters in the benched home ends were far from quiet but their attempts to drown out the noise of their rivals were doomed to fail as the buzz that had been growing since October reached crescendo.

"I'm sure it's affecting both sets of players," said MacPherson in reference to the atmosphere, "but oblivious to it all is referee Bill Crombie from Edinburgh." Crombie, a well-known Hearts fan, was a controversial choice as official for such a big game and, on the sound of his whistle, his team began their date with destiny.

The favourites, decked out in their silver away kit, thought they were about to take another giant stride towards the title within the opening 20 minutes. Sandy Clark took control of the ball by the stand-side touchline and turned Colin Hendry before bursting into the box. Having carried the ball too close to the goaline to be thinking about a shot, Clark was assessing his options when the chasing Hendry, playing one of his first games in central defence, clearly barged the striker over before wrapping his foot around the ball. Ten-thousand Jambos in the crowd, 11 on the pitch and several more in the dugout screamed for a penalty but referee Crombie was unimpressed. Dundee fans and players, as well as anyone of a Celtic persuasion following proceedings, breathed a sigh of relief.

"It was a definite penalty," said Mike Smith, who witnessed the incident from behind the goal. "I couldn't believe he never gave it. I still can't."

If that wasn't bad enough, Jambos' hopes of a shock at Love Street had taken a dent. It had taken Celtic only six minutes to break the deadlock. An inswinging corner from Owen Archdeacon was met by the head of Brian McClair and the ball looped over goalkeeper Jim Stewart and into the net. Any nerves they may have been feeling eased as the players ran back to the centre circle to begin their assault on the St Mirren goal anew and as many as 15,000 of the 17,000 crowd roared their approval. The goal had come against the run of play as St Mirren had actually started the stronger of the two teams and had passed up three chances before Celtic scored, with Peter Mackie guilty of passing up a particularly gilt-edged opportunity. This meant the game plan Alex Miller and his players had worked on all week had to be ripped up almost as soon as the game had started. "We expected a bit of an onslaught but we also thought they would be nervous so the plan was to take the game to them from the start," said Fitzpatrick. "People forget that we started the game well and had a couple of really good chances to get the first goal but we didn't and it wasn't long before Celtic scored."

"Once the game started we settled after a couple of scares and the early goal really lifted the crowd," said Eddie Toner. "From then on people were even more confident we'd do our bit."

At Easter Road, Hibees were ambivalent about events on the park and seemed apathetic about a Mark Fulton own goal handing Dundee United the lead. Never had an end of season game been so meaningless and rarely had events elsewhere been so packed with implication. Watching their team half-heartedly see out the season while waiting for grim news from elsewhere to be confirmed was a excruciating form of punishment for the Hibees who did decide to brave Easter Road that day.

"It was a poor game, typical end of season stuff, nothing much to get excited about," said John Craig. "No one was glued to transistors as far as I could see. It wasn't as if we believed it was possible."

Back at Dens, Hearts continued to endeavour without ever seriously troubling Bobby Geddes' goal or coming close the fluency that had marked out much of their play throughout their remarkable run. The first-half was a nervy, stop-start affair characterised by misplaced passes and needless fouls as Dundee, too, struggled to find any kind of rhythm or to fashion chances. With only a point required to secure the title this was hardly a disaster for Hearts and down on the Dundee bench Albert Kidd felt he would see out the season, possibly his last in the country, as a spectator.

"I thought that something dramatic needed to happen before I'd get on," he said. "I didn't think there was much chance I'd feature at all. Even though I was on the bench I wasn't really feeling like I was part of things at that stage."

After McClair had given them the lead, Celtic had continued to press forward and their efforts paid off in a spectacular six-minute period. First, Maurice Johnston ran on to a perfectly weighted through ball from Paul McStay to finish before doubling his total almost from the restart. Facing his own goal and with St Mirren attackers bearing down on him inside his own penalty area, Danny McGrain coolly flipped the ball over his head and straight to Murdo MacLeod, who knocked it first time to McStay on the right touchline. The man Celtic fans called 'Maestro' turned inside and laid the ball off to captain Roy Aitken, who played it into the path of the now advancing McGrain. Spotting McClair ahead of him, the veteran full back didn't bother taking a touch before feeding the striker who nutmegged St Mirren's Neil Cooper and drove to the corner of the penalty box before squaring it for Johnston to slide home at the back post. Commentator Jock Brown, future Celtic General Manager, instantly labelled it "one of the goals of the season" and Celtic fans still regard it as one of the best their team has ever scored. It was a stunning display of precision and movement, the type of goal that has coaches weak at the knees as they see the drills practiced day in, day out executed perfectly on the big occasion. Celtic now knew any win for Dundee would see them clinch the title but they were far from finished and the ball was in the net again five minutes later when Murdo MacLeod cleverly dummied an Archdeacon pass to allow McStay to smash the ball into the roof of the net from inside the six-yard box.

Davie Hay says he stood on the touchline in awe of his own team during that first half, while Jock Brown said there was, "no question about it, Celtic are certainly playing like champions." News of Celtic's demolition was also starting to spread round the country.

"The first I heard news from either game was that Celtic were 3-0 up," said Hibee John Craig. "Then at half time it was four. No one had really been interested but suddenly we were looking at each other thinking, 'you never know. If we need two impossible things to fall into place then that's one of them. It puts pressure on them and they might get nervous'. For the first time we were thinking 'maybe'. Then we reasoned that Hearts were 0-0. That was good enough for them and they would likely hold on. I don't remember people feverishly trying for updates from Dens. I don't even know where the news came from."

The knowledge that their advantage in goal difference had been wiped out ratcheted up the tension Jambos were feeling by several notches as news started to spread around the Dens Park terraces, as Mike Smith remembered. "The fella in front of me was nearly embroiled in a fight when he relayed the news to irritated Hearts fans that Celtic were four goals ahead at half time. They thought he was taking the piss. That was the first sign that nerves were starting to get to the crowd."

"There was a noticeable change in atmosphere just a couple of minutes before half time," said Barry Davidson, watching the game from the opposite end of the ground. "There were no smart phones getting you the latest scores so more often than not the first you were aware of other games was over tannoy at half time. I was just desperate to hear that Rangers were losing and there was the odd punter with a radio but the two biggest stories were happening at Dens and Love Street so news from Ibrox was scarce.

"I remember distinctly being told by someone that Celtic were four-up that day whilst standing at the pie stall. Right away, Dundee fans started goading Hearts supporters across the railings. I remember looking across to them and there was a bit of defiance but you genuinely knew what they were thinking."

As the players made their way up the tunnel, a Hearts fan in the enclosure stretched out towards keeper Henry Smith and made him aware that Celtic were 4-0 up at Love Street, clearly believing that the knowledge would spur his teammates on to victory in the second-half. He needn't have bothered as the Hearts management team were already aware of the situation at Love Street as chief scout, Ian Cruickshanks had been instructed to attend the match and keep MacDonald and co informed of developments via a proto-portable phone that took up a not-inconsiderable space on the ground next to their bench. "Needless to say, Ian didn't bother calling after the interval," was how Doddie remembered his first encounter with cellular telecommunications in his autobiography.

"I knew they were winning handsomely because we could hear the news being relayed to their bench," said Kidd. "John McCormack was the other sub and 'Cowboy' was a right Celtic supporter. He was saying to me, 'Celtic are killing St Mirren' – and he was a former St Mirren player! But we weren't affected by it. We were playing for Europe – but to do it when you're playing for the league championship, it wasn't something I would have done myself. I was conscious of them knowing what was going on. I thought it was a silly move, and maybe distracting for the players, who might have been looking to the radio for updates."

Hearts' hosts also had bad news waiting for them as they reached their dressing room. Rangers had taken the lead with a Dave MacPherson goal on the stroke of half time. A Motherwell win was looking increasingly unlikely so the Dark Blues' only hope was to win both points and hope the Steelmen could grab an equaliser. Dundee's fans were not confident at that point, and indeed the club's tannoy announcer urged Hearts fans to stay off the pitch at the end of the game to allow the championship trophy to be presented. "Well, that must mean the PA man has a crystal ball," remarked Archie in the TV gantry above Dundee's vociferous 'Derry'. "We'll see."

As rumour and counter-rumour swirled around the country, Celtic were initially dealt a blow at the interval, as Murdo MacLeod recalls: "When we went in at half-time someone said that Dundee were 1-0 up and we were thinking 'fantastic' but within seconds we were told it was still 0-0. Initially we were disappointed but then still happy that Hearts weren't winning. We still had a chance."

On the Love Street terraces, the fans were considerably better informed than the players. In his match report, Ron Scott noted that "this was the day that ten thousand transistor batteries went flat as just about every Celtic fan had a radio at Love Street." Indeed, he acknowledges that the press box was also dependent on the Celtic support for news from Dundee. "The press guys rarely had access to a radio in this pre-mobile phone era. We were relying on fans to keep us informed and worked out what was happening by the reaction of the crowd. The fact there had been no roar and the atmosphere remained upbeat led us to think it was still 0-0."

Seven miles east of Love Street, MacPherson's goal had lifted the gloom brought about by a dire first half coupled with the news that Celtic were hammering St Mirren and were only a Dundee goal, which they already dreaded for their own reasons, from winning a league that looked to be beyond them only weeks ago. Graeme Souness had received a rapturous reception from the 21,500 crowd when he and

Walter Smith were introduced before the game but his first match as Rangers manager could hardly have inspired him so far. Indeed, James Traynor, one day to become Rangers' communications director but for now still a newspaper reporter, commented that "had he [Souness] wanted to find a quiet corner where he could bang his head against a wall it would be understandable. What he had witnessed was not at all that to which he has become accustomed."

"The whole game was a bit surreal," recalled Rangers supporter Hamish Strachan. "There were people obviously looking for a Rangers victory for ourselves to make sure we got into Europe but there were a lot listening to their radios for the Hearts score. Them winning would obviously have been the ideal result as it meant us qualifying for Europe and Celtic missing out on the league but the priority for me was Rangers winning and us qualifying on our own steam.

"You started getting updates. 'It's 1-0 Celtic, it's 2-0, 3-0 now' and people were saying 'don't tell me it's going to go wrong now'. The more goals Celtic got the more worried people were getting. There started to be angry accusations about St Mirren lying down and letting them win the league and I'm sure the same thing was being said in the Hearts crowd as well. St Mirren were being called for all sorts.

"It was still up to Hearts though, that's the way we saw it. It was at the back of peoples' minds what the score was and updates kept coming through and you couldn't help but get dragged into it. Like I say, I was first and foremost concerned about Rangers but there were definitely some fans far more concerned by what was going on at Love Street and Dens and would have swapped our European qualification to stop Celtic winning the league if they were offered. You always get those bitter people in any support but, for me, getting to Europe was a must for a club like Rangers and that's what I was bothered about."

All told, few supporters of Premier Division sides could be said to be enjoying themselves as the teams re-emerged for the final 45 minutes of the season with the country gripped by tension. Hearts still had one hand on the league trophy but news from Love Street meant their journey to the title was akin to walking a tightrope. Having put their game beyond doubt and having their hopes raised exponentially, Celtic fans were now absorbed by what was happening in Dundee, where the home fans tried to come to terms with the likelihood of their cherished European ambition coming to nought. St Mirren supporters were enduring the thrashing they feared and of the diehards that turned up that day many had already abandoned the game before the half-time whistle. Hibee stomachs remained in knots at the prospect of their arch-enemy clinching the league. The delight that had accompanied Celtic's onslaught was tempered by the realisation that Hearts only needed to repeat the trick of the first half and stop Dundee scoring to make that elusive league title theirs. Would Hearts twist or stick?

"There was a lot of tension on the terraces from the moment the teams came back out," said Mike Smith. "The performance and atmosphere deteriorated. We just wanted it to be over and to get the party started in earnest. It was the longest half imaginable. We tried to calm our nerves with the belief that it didn't matter if Celtic scored ten goals, as long as Hearts secured the single point needed for glory. Although the Hearts players were collectively having a poor game, we still believed they would get this point."

In his book, *Manchester United Ruined My Life*, the lifelong Manchester City supporter Colin Schindler candidly discusses his antipathy towards their rivals. Noting that passion for sport defies logic, he admits that he will "do anything in my power to create a defeat for Manchester United", sentiments that would have had fans of Hibernian nodding in agreement as 1985/86 drew to a conclusion. There was not a Hibs fan among the disappointing crowd of less than 4000 at Easter Road that didn't wish the 63rd minute penalty their side equalised from had been awarded 70 miles north and greeted with apoplexy from Hearts sympathisers everywhere. Polite applause rang out as scorer Steve Cowan and his team mates jogged back to their own half for the re-start but in terms of palliative care it did nothing to ease the Hibees' agony.

Football grounds across Scotland appeared to be operating in a different time dimension from the rest of the universe. Watches were checked with increased regularity. Radio owners were badgered for updates. Terraces were paced. Aside from those at the game, hundreds of thousands of people across the country were now keeping track of the drama via radio, Grandstand's videprinter or other means. Whatever their loyalties and whatever result they craved, all who tuned in watched the time tick slowly by waiting for news from Dens Park, where, as it turned out, something was afoot.

"It was a bit of a surprise when Archie turned to me and said, 'you're going on,'" said Albert Kidd. "Tosh

McKinlay had done his knee. Otherwise I might never have got on. The manager obviously had to reshape the team because he's a left back. I'm pretty sure Archie was telling me to get my defensive duties right and get at them when I could. And that's what happened."

The change took place in the 61st minute, around 15 minutes before word of a Motherwell equaliser swept round the home end, galvanising the Dark Blues' players and supporters alike. "The Derry broke into cheering and celebrating with news that Rangers had lost a goal," said Barry Davidson. "It swept around the ground and a few minutes went by with us believing a goal would clinch Europe. I believe that news filtered through to the players. A draw was no good to DFC. We had to win and Hearts didn't and that was definitely being reflected on the pitch."

In reality, the Dark Blues were destined for disappointment. Their informant proved unreliable and, although there had indeed been a goal in Govan, it was for the home side. Referee Alistair Huett awarded the type of penalty that non-Old Firm fans contend are only given to the home side at Ibrox and Celtic Park when Ted McMinn went down under an innocuous challenge from Motherwell's Graeme Forbes. Ally McCoist tucked the penalty away to secure his team's place in Europe and edge past Brian McClair to become the country's top marksman for that season.

Regardless of how many Dundee fans learned the truth of the Ibrox scoreline, the news never filtered through to the team. Believing they still had a chance of playing in the following season's UEFA Cup they continued to attack Hearts, who were either content to soak up pressure and hit on the break or were forced into the strategy by Dundee's pressing, and their own nerves and fatigue.

One man clearly not affected by nerves or fatigue was Albert Kidd. For all his protestations about lacking an engine, Kidd seemed to be in possession of a boundless supply of energy as he charged about the field like a man possessed. One moment he was dropping deep to link the midfield and attack before making a run beyond the Hearts defence, the next he was making a vital tackle deep in his own half. He would be darting up the wing chasing what should have been a lost cause before popping up as a de facto sweeper to mop up a rare Jambos attack seconds later. Wherever the action was, Albert Kidd was there as well. Wherever the ball was on the field, he was guaranteed to be in the vicinity fighting for it, making a mockery of the positional awareness Knox and Scott put such store in but also buzzing around his opponents and forcing them to deal with a new, unorthodox and dangerously unpredictable threat.

At Love Street, it was a familiar foe in Brian McClair that had scored his second, and his side's fifth, early in the second half but the atmosphere turned decidedly eerie thereafter. The longer time went with no news of a Dundee goal, the more it appeared the excellent performance had been in vain. Energy levels of fans and players alike dipped. For the team, it was a case of going through the motions for the remaining half-hour while, on the terraces, rain that had persisted all afternoon fell heavier on bodies no longer inoculated by the first-half performance and pre-match libations that were fading.

It was too little too late, thought Celts as they rued dropped points, defensive mistakes, missed chances and refereeing errors throughout the season. Just one penalty given or not, or a single deflection spinning one way instead of the other could have left them savouring this moment rather than hoping against hope that something, anything, would happen in Dundee.

"When we went 5-0 up then all we wanted to do was make sure we didn't concede a goal," admitted Murdo MacLeod. "We knew that if they nicked one then another then there would be nerves and a danger everything we'd done to that point was for nothing. I understand everything going flat but we had been incredible in that first half and had to be because St Mirren worked as hard as any team could and made us earn it."

"It was one of the strangest halves of football I've ever seen," remembered St Mirren supporter Mac-Donald. "Neither team wanted to do anything. Celtic had done their job and didn't want to do anything to put that at risk but there wasn't much chance of that as we just wanted it all finished."

"Time was marching on, we were happy to play out a brilliant 5- 0 win, Hearts were happy to sit on a 0-0," said Paul Larkin. "Amidst all the tension I turned and saw a guy standing next to me in the full Don Johnson Miami Vice rig out. He even had his sleeves rolled up in his all white suit with turquoise t-shirt. He was getting soaked and increasingly pissed off as the suit was shrinking."

For Hearts fans not unable to make the Dens Park showdown, the feeling of impotence was even more pronounced than it was on the terraces. In *Two Miles to Tynecastle*, his memoir of a troubled childhood, Jambo Andrew-Henry Bowie recalled how it felt to be alone with only the radio for company on that afternoon: "The commentator was becoming more and more animated. As the minutes ticked on, it seemed that Hearts were now hanging on for dear life. The tension was unbearable and I became gripped with fear, like I was going to be sick. I became frantic, and began ferociously pacing around, clutching my hair, pulling at it, begging for the end."

On the Dens Park terraces, nails were being bitten beyond the quick, chests thumped and pulses could be heard as the adrenaline coursing round their bodies caused knees to weaken. Hearts goalkeeper Henry Smith remembers spending the entire second half glancing at the clock in the corner of Dens Park. "Twenty past four, half past four. Has it stopped?" It was a feeling he shared with those on the terraces. Just fifteen minutes more. Please God, please. Twelve minutes. Colquhoun missed a chance. Ten minutes to go. Great save from Smith. Please. Come on Hearts. We've come so far. Thirty-one games unbeaten. We've waited for this all our lives. So near. Nine minutes. We deserve it. Eight minutes now. Then it happened.

Kidd picked the ball up wide on the right. Substitute Kenny Black, playing at left-back in place of the afflicted Whittaker, cut off his path inside, trying to force him wide but backing off rather than making a challenge. Moving infield 20 yards from goal, Kidd shimmied one way then the other but his opponent didn't buy it. Kidd then knocked the ball forward, far enough away from the back-peddling Black to wrap his foot around it and get a low cross in that evaded the Hearts' player's outstretched boot. Lacking pace and power, the cross was nonetheless dangerous enough to force the covering Roddy MacDonald to clear at the front post ahead of the inrushing Graham Harvey. Dundee had a corner. The elegant Robert Connor effortlessly whipped a high ball into the box with his cultured left foot. It dipped toward the penalty box where John Brown leapt high above the Hearts defence to direct the ball towards the back post. For any team, the marking was slack. For a rock solid Hearts team that hadn't lost a goal at a corner all season it was unbelievable. Albert Kidd had stolen past his static marker and found himself in hectares of space as he instinctively swung his boot at Brown's knock-down and drove the ball high into the far corner of the goal. The Jambos' descent from purgatory to hell had begun.

"I had just checked my watch for the hundredth time that afternoon," said Mike Smith. "When Kidd scored we were just frozen to the spot. It was a few seconds before anyone did anything other than stare in shock. The massed ranks of Hearts fans stood motionless, as if time had stopped. Our world certainly had. As the disconsolate Hearts players made their way to the centre circle to re-start the game, I shouted 'C'mon Hearts – we can still do this!' I was a lone voice – in our heart of hearts, we knew the dream was over."

The goalscorer wheeled away to take the adulation of his team-mates and the Dundee fans dancing on their benches, clearly believing European qualification was possible. "It was celebrated like any late goal in a must-win game at a packed ground," said

Dark Blues fan Barry Davidson. "Dundee had their own aims for that day and that was to finish above Rangers. Of course there were surges towards the railings to wind-up Hearts fans but it was all about us winning and keeping our season's goal alive."

A few seconds later the news reached Love Street, Easter Road and Ibrox via the transistor radios that had finally come up trumps. Initially there was confusion as the commentator's excited announcement that "Kidd has scored!" was passed on verbatim, leading many to believe that Hearts' better-known Walter and not Albert had broken the deadlock.

Cheering quickly died away at Ibrox when the truth dawned on the Gers' fans, but waves of euphoria swept over Love Street and Easter Road. Hibs' winger Joe Tortolano was left bemused by the eruption that greeted his throw-in while St Mirren goalkeeper Jim Stewart, a former Rangers player, took a cross at the second attempt, confusion, perhaps even disappointment, etched across his face, as the Celtic fans behind him roared and danced with wild abandon. The black and white army had been steadily marching through the five stages of grief in the second half, tramping beyond denial and anger shortly after Celtic's fifth. Having patrolled past bargaining and depression, they were fast approaching acceptance by the time Kidd struck.

"And that must be a goal for Dundee," said Jock Brown trying to make sense of the melee on the terraces. "Sheer bedlam around the stadium. Dundee have clearly scored at Dens and it's lift-off here at Love Street. What incredible scenes."

"The whole stadium erupted," remembered Eddie

Toner. "We wanted confirmation so we asked a guy in front of us with a radio to his ear what was going on. He looked puzzled – 'What's going on where?' 'At Dundee, where else?' I fired back. 'I've no idea pal, I'm listening to this game!' We couldn't believe it."

"After the initial confusion came sheer delirium," said fellow Celtic supporter Paul Larkin. "It was so late in the game that you'd all but given up hope of anything good happening at Dens and suddenly you were being told it had. We danced around the back of the mudheap terrace going crazy and starting to believe that we could be champions."

Watching the Celtic fans celebrate this dramatic turn of events from the home end was David Mac-Donald. "I'll never forget that wall of noise that went up when news came through that Albert Kidd had scored," he said. "I can't think of another time I heard a noise quite like that one. I've heard louder when a goal has been scored in the game I was watching but it was such a strange situation that there's never been anything like that."

"Until my dying day I will always remember the shock I felt," recalled Celtic goalkeeper Pat Bonner in his autobiography, *The Last Line*. "An explosion of sound suddenly roared out from behind Jim Stewart and then, like a huge wave from different groups around the stadium, until it came from every single Celtic supporter in the ground. The hairs on the back of my neck stood to attention as I took in the news, the only news it could be – that Dundee had scored at Dens Park."

His teammate Murdo MacLeod remained cautious, however. "We were comfortable in our game and you were wondering what was happening at the other game, listening for clues, changes in the atmosphere etc. We knew there wasn't long left in our game, how long was left at Dens? Then there was a phenomenal noise from the crowd and you thought Dundee must've scored. We wouldn't necessarily have known if Hearts had taken the lead already though, so it might have been an equaliser for all we knew. We were all on the pitch trying to work out what was happening. You thought 'it must be' but you couldn't be sure."

At Easter Road there was carnage on the terraces, as Hibee John Craig remembered. "There were only about 3500 there that day but the ground absolutely erupted. One of the guys I was with fell to his knees, shaking and screaming, eyes wide in ecstasy, veins bulging out of his neck. I've never seen someone go that colour of red before and you honestly thought his veins might explode."

At Love Street Celtic's manager Davie Hay could be seen appealing for calm from the dugout. There were still seven minutes to play. A Hearts equaliser now would make Celtic's failure even more painful and cruel than it had been 60 seconds earlier.

But back at Dens there was only one team looking likely to add to the scoreline. Hearts' attempts to attack were easily repelled by the Dundee defence and the away team looked beaten as they tried to get the ball forward with little thought or finesse. With legs rested for much of the league campaign, Albert wasn't ready to sign off for the summer just yet.

There were only three minutes of the season left when Albert Kidd collected the ball, just inside his half, near the right touchline. With his first touch he flew past Kenny Black and cut inside, 30 yards from goal with Gary Mackay in his wake. Driving towards the penalty box, Kidd lifted his head and slipped the ball to Graham Harvey on the 18-yard-line. The shellshocked Hearts players failed to track his run as Albert met Harvey's return pass first time and lashed the ball home.

Some Hearts fans collapsed in agony, others, over-taken by nervous energy and anger, spilled on to the track, baying for the blood of the man who was now sprinting the length of the Derry with his arm aloft to take its acclaim. Albert Kidd had fulfilled a boyhood dream by winning the league for Celtic, without ever playing for them. Furthermore he had cost Hearts a league that destiny appeared to have promised them. A player who had spent much of his career in the lower leagues, who had failed to live up to expecta-tions after his big move, whose time at Dens had been blighted by injuries and a crisis of confidence, who had failed to score in a season in which he hardly featured and who was so out-of-favour that only an 11th-hour appeal to his manager saw him sneak a place on the bench, had written his name in the history books. He had delivered untold misery to some and brought unbridled joy to others. In just seven minutes he had altered the lives of hundreds of thousands of people across Scotland and beyond.

Not being present to witness it didn't make the hammer blow any less painful for Andrew-Henry Bowie. "I sank to the floor and screamed," he said. "I sobbed uncontrollably, more than at any other time in my life, face down and sprawled on the carpet. I'd lived through some dire domestic situations and seen dreams dashed many times before and since. But this was the worst moment ever."

The significance of Kidd's double was not lost on Dundee fans like Barry Davidson, disappointed as they were by the real scoreline from Ibrox. "I'm 95 per cent certain that in the gap between first and second goals the majority of people around me had realised that Rangers were winning and not losing and it would be a hollow victory and another season of so near yet so far. It was disappointing but you knew you were watching something huge, something that was bigger than DFC missing out on a couple of European games."

Already Kidd's legend was being written in Leith. If the scenes that accompanied Kidd's opener on the terraces were joyous, they were nothing compared to the reaction to his clincher. The eruption was such that there could be no doubt about the fact Hearts had lost out on the league and the team's attention was diverted from the game at hand, allowing Stuart Beedie to drift into the penalty area largely unimpeded and win the game for United.

"It's that twisted pleasure you get watching rivals suffer," said John Craig. "When the ground exploded again we knew there was no time for them to equalise now. No one had any interest in the Hibs game by now. We knew we wouldn't hear the celebrations of Jambos that night. It was then I thought it was a great time to be at Easter Road amongst like-minded people. To be honest, it's slightly grim how good it felt. It's not quite right but it's the stuff that keeps you going through the dark times."

If no one of a Hibs persuasion cared how their own

game panned out, Hamish Strachan remembers the situation and feelings being more complicated at Ibrox. "I'm not saying I wasn't disappointed to see Celtic win the league but ultimately I went to that game to support Rangers and desperately wanted them to win the game and get into Europe. If Celtic won the league, so be it, you take it on the chin and look after yourselves.

"We heard Dundee had scored and there was a fair bit of discontent because we knew the league was over but, at the same time, it had the strange effect of pulling our attention back to the Rangers game because there was no point worrying about Celtic or Hearts anymore. We couldn't do anything stupid to lose our lead and in the end the players were clapped off the park."

David MacDonald doesn't recall much of a reaction to news of Kidd's second goal as the Celtic fans were still celebrating his first but Paul Larkin remembers it differently. "We got the news the second one had gone in and suddenly that was it, we were champions. After seeing Celtic play as well as I'd ever seen them play, before or since, we'd pipped Hearts right at the death and had the league. Grown men cried and, as I turned round to look for the people I was with, there was Don Johnson lying on top of the mudheap, suit completely ruined, going crazy, this time at what he'd seen and heard."

The full-time whistle at Love Street didn't come until a minute or so after the end of the Dundee-Hearts game, leaving Celtic supporters to blithely ignore the tannoy announcer's pleas to stay off the pitch in the knowledge they were officially the champions of

Scotland. As the Celtic players rushed to the tunnel they were accosted by teammates and staff from the bench, as well as fans, who furnished them with the pertinent details. Dundee had won 2-0. Albert Kidd? Really?

"When the full-time whistle went I still didn't know if the Dundee-Hearts game had finished and was trying to find someone to confirm it," said Murdo MacLeod. "It was Danny McGrain who told me it was 2-0 and, as the fans were pouring on to the pitch, you realised it must have finished at Dens."

Among those who ran from the terraces was Eddie Toner. "It was the only time I ever invaded the pitch," he laughed. "Everyone started pouring on and you were just totally caught up in the moment." After a party on the pitch lasting almost 15 minutes, the Celtic supporters were cleared back to the terraces to allow their heroes to re-emerge from the changing room for a well-deserved, if unexpected, lap of honour. Players and fans celebrated as one as poor performances and abuse from the Jungle were forgotten and Hay breathed a sigh of relief, knowing his job was safe for the time being. A Celtic team regarded as falling far below the standard expected at that giant club had just delivered one of the most memorable moments in their history. Regardless of the intervention of Mr Kidd, nothing should detract from the resolve Celtic showed to recover from a seemingly hopeless position to become league champions with an exceptional second half of the season, which saw them overcome all setbacks and rise to the challenges put in front of them.

Knowing how their rivals would be reacting at that

exact moment no doubt intensified the Jambos' feelings of despair as the full-time whistle sounded at Dens and their dreams were officially ended. Fans ran from both home and away ends and minor skirmishes broke out on the pitch before police and stewards stepped in to quickly restore order. Hundreds of Hearts fans then made their way across the pitch to commiserate with their heroes and thank them for their exceptional efforts that until seven minutes ago had looked enough to earn a first league title for 26 years. Some stood frozen to the spot while others hurried to the exit, unable to stand the scene of their glorious failure a second longer. Some sung Hearts songs in defiance while more slumped to the ground, unable to believe what had just happened. Grown men cried and held on to each other for support as their fellow Jambos rolled around the terraces, track or pitch, incapable of controlling their grief. Glory had been snatched away from them at the last and already they knew they would never get over the pain they felt at that moment.

"I've probably averaged around 30 Dundee games per season in the 30 years since then so you tend forget far more than you remember but that is one scene you couldn't forget," said Barry Davidson. "There were guys totally ruined. There was some scuffling outside as we exited so that slowed the crowd down leaving and I was left standing watching for a few minutes. It was classic car crash viewing. You were looking at it but felt you probably shouldn't be. Just leave them to it. But you couldn't take your eyes off it."

Football writer Roddy Forsyth was another watching very different post-match action to what he had envisaged. The enduring memory for him was an "elderly couple rocking back and forth in their seats as they hugged each other close in silent consolation. At their age, they had experienced a world war and, no doubt, significant and painful personal losses. In that moment, though, they were embroiled in the derailed fortunes of their football team."

Forsyth noted that the couple no doubt remembered similar scenes in 1965. Had goal difference been in play then Hearts would have been champions. Had the Tynecastle side not petitioned for a change in tie-breaking criteria and goal average still applied, they would have won the league 21 years later. "Such is the mesmerising capacity of football to elevate and torment," he concluded.

The scene of devastation that was the away end at Dens Park that afternoon epitomised the cruelty of football; melodramatic to outsiders but understood perfectly well by the initiated. Knowing just how much pain the Jambos – some friends, colleagues and relatives – would be going through made the moment all the sweeter for Hibees.

The despair was not confined to supporters either. "Under normal circumstances, at the end of the season, you'd ask the players to go back out and go to the supporters who've supported them," reflected chairman Wallace Mercer later. "But in those circumstances quite rightly you couldn't ask them to do that." In their stead, Mercer went out to greet the Hearts fans and waved a maroon scarf around his head. It was not the glorious climax to the season that everyone at Tynecastle had expected.

"I remember everyone lying around and the supporters being on the pitch," said John Colquhoun. "It's hard now, still, to think about it. You can still see their faces. There's nothing else in football that would ever feel like that. Ever. There's only people who've gone through that would know what that dressing room was like."

His teammate John Robertson agreed that it was hard to imagine "how low, how drained, how empty that you felt. You felt you'd let anyone who'd ever supporter Hearts down" while Gary Mackay remarked that "the last eight minutes will live with Hearts supporters and players for the rest of their lives."

He continued. "We took the supporters along the road when we're looking to succeed together to give Heart of Midlothian pride back because it's lost a lot over the previous 20-30 years. Unfortunately we weren't able to deliver and that's something we all live with."

Having been made aware that Rangers had beaten Motherwell after all, the Dundee players' cup was hardly overflowing with joy either, particularly for those whose allegiances lay on the opposite side of the Old Firm divide to Kidd's. "Everyone was totally committed to Dundee and we were a bit disappointed because we missed out on Europe but you couldn't help processing what it meant for the team you supported. Bomber was not happy, but a few of us were Celtic supporters and Graham Harvey, as an ex-Hibs player, was happy how things had turned out as well. I remember Archie sitting across from me in the dressing room, and he really was not that happy. 'Fuck's sake wee man,' he said. I asked him if he was happy that we won and he said, 'Well aye, but what a fucking situation you've put us in,' before adding that he was distraught for Hearts.

"I was obviously feeling rosy and pink about the whole thing but he looked pretty stunned. He never sat down in the dressing room much, but he was sitting down then, right across from me. I remember being on a flight with Archie to Germany. The plane hit a bit of turbulence. He looked at me and I was like, 'Do this, boss' and crossed myself. He said 'Nah, look at my surname. Knox. I can't do that.' Maybe that had something to do with it!

"I remember seeing Alex MacDonald walking off the pitch aware he had lost the league. You couldn't not feel for him. The aftermath was incredible. The impromptu press conference was held outside the dressing room door and the first thing I saw was John Robertson and Gary Mackay, both in tears. I didn't know what to do other than apologise to them but neither answered. The disappointment on all the Hearts' players and supporters' faces wasn't nice. I felt for them."

The contrast between Dens Park and Love Street could hardly have been more marked. "There are defining moments in football and in life when you realise the gods are smiling on you," said Hay. "This was undoubtedly such an occasion. In the run-in, I believed Hearts would slip up somewhere along the line. I had witnessed it countless times before and I had to believe that they might not get the bounce of the ball in at least one game."

The party in Celtic's dressing room would almost have met with the approval of the temperance movement, as Bill Morrison of the *Sunday Mail* noted in his match report. "Celtic are the new Premier League champions after one of the greatest smash-and-grab acts in the competition's history," he wrote. "And it appeared that Celtic's fifth Premier title and 34th League Championship triumph caught even the Parkhead club by surprise – they took only one bottle of champagne with them to Love Street. Grinning broadly, manager Davie Hay emerged from the bedlam of the dressing room to say: 'I'm afraid we only brought one bottle of champagne and that isn't going to last long. I reckon we'll need to break into an off-license on the way home!'"

Celtic hadn't wanted to pre-empt a celebration that most of the nation believed wouldn't happen and the solitary bottle of fizz was produced from the magic bag of Jimmy Steele – the club's masseur who had obviously shared Hay's unshakable belief in his side.

While the away dressing room at Love Street hosted a celebration, a wake was taking place next door, according to Tony Fitzpatrick. "It was honestly one of the worst I've ever felt after a game. It was absolutely horrible in that dressing room, hearing Celtic players celebrate next door and their supporters outside the window. You have professional pride and you never want to get beat on your own patch, let alone have someone take the piss and win the league there."

Back at Dens, Alex MacDonald had tried three times to face his players only for his emotions to let him down. Finally he was able to control the tears that flowed in the away bathroom and returned to the dressing room, where he thanked the Hearts team for everything they had done that season.

"Among the first things to hit me at the time was

that, with our Scottish Cup Final against Aberdeen only a week away, I'd to try and lift the players' spirits. But I couldn't do it because I started to fill up with tears. I went into the toilet, spoke to myself, and resolved to try again. Still, I couldn't do it. Finally, I was able to tell the players to think about what they'd achieved in taking the title race to the last day – and with a big day at Hampden looming, what they could achieve still. Those Hearts fans who had made the trip to Dens with such high expectations were as distraught as the rest of us. In truth, I've never quite come to terms with how the title was snatched away from us in such dire circumstances."

One unenviable task completed, there were another group the shattered Tynecastle boss had to face. "It's very hard to talk," he told the waiting press pack. "We had five players suffering from a virus all week. There's little more I want to say at this time."

In the age of Sky Sports and saturation-level live coverage, fans are accustomed to seeing league tables updated in real time in the corner of our screens each time a goal is scored. Had such a facility existed on May 3rd 1986 it wouldn't have shown the lead swinging one way then the other. Hearts had topped the table from 4.45pm on December 21st the previous year until the 83rd minute of the final day of the season but that was seven minutes too soon. The places at the top of the league changed only once that day, enough to end their dream and ensure a tear-stained trip home, where jubilant Hibees would be waiting to greet them.

"I'll be honest, I didn't go to Easter Road that day," said Colin Christie. "Couldn't face it. I hadn't even checked the score all afternoon and was just thinking about putting the radio on when my mate phoned to say Dundee had scored. I listened to the rest of the game and was going daft in the living room when they scored again. That was us on it for the night."

John Craig was also in a celebratory mood as confirmation of Heart's plight was confirmed. "I came out of the game absolutely delighted and couldn't wait for Sportscene. It's one of my abiding memories, watching how stunned the Hearts fans were at Dens. Them sitting on the wee wall shocked, not knowing what had happened. That was the days of video tapes and I watched it over and over looking for someone I knew but never saw anyone. I still had that tape amongst my Hibs ones after video was obsolete."

For Jambo Bobby Mitchell, the trip back to Edinburgh passed in stunned silence. "I'd been drinking all day and got more for the journey down the road but no matter how hard I tried, I couldn't get drunk and couldn't shift the mood. I'd actually tried to storm out when Dundee scored their second but everyone was frozen to the spot on the terraces and I couldn't get past them. I had to watch it all unfold. Then the bus back was fucking horrible. Kids were crying all the way home."

"Our plans to go out in Perth were abandoned," said fellow Hearts fan Mike Smith. "A relatively short journey home to Aberdeen turned into the longest trip in the world. My mate and I sat on the bus back to the Granite City and said nothing to each other. On arrival in Aberdeen, we went for a quick pint but our sombre mood didn't call for alcohol, particularly as more than one smart alec in the pub noticed our crumpled Hearts scarves sticking out our pockets and made a less than sympathetic comment.

"I made my way home and my wife at the time greeted me with the news she thought she felt our first baby might be on its way. Selfishly and to my eternal shame, I ignored her and headed for bed. It was 7.30pm on a Saturday night and I just wanted the world to end. It was one of the most traumatic experiences of my life, only surpassed by the sudden death of my father in 1997."

Precious few mementos of the biggest day of Albert Kidd's career remain. The Dundee kitman was not someone who gave away the strips he was responsible for lightly while the boots that broke hearts ended up in a heap on the floor for cleaning, lost in a sea of others.

The man who had inflicted such misery on Hearts believes that the fact he was actually playing out of position during his brief but spectacular cameo adds insult to injury for Hearts fans.

"I came on against Hearts on the right," he said. "It wasn't really my position. I remember when the first goal went in, they went to sleep. They shut down. Normally you wouldn't skip past players the way I did. Normally you wouldn't do that if they were really on song.

"They had switched off completely by then. They were thinking about not losing the league rather than concentrating on their job. I know from my own career the impact that the mental side, confidence, concentration and pressure has on your performance. Archie used to say to drag the ball to the side of the full back and try to get a cross in because I was good at that rather than knocking it past the full back and running on to it. I shouldn't have been able to get past Kenny Black like that.

"Don't get me wrong, I was out to win the game for Dundee for our own reasons but I'd be lying if I said it wasn't at the back of my mind Celtic had won the league as I celebrated the second goal. When I was coming on I was probably thinking that if I did well then I might get some interest in the summer. It wasn't a surprise for me what happened because I knew what I was capable of if I was employed correctly.

"I was always one for the big occasion. Over the years I'd played really well in bigger games and can remember getting named man of the match when I came up against Paul McStay at Dens. I would rise to the occasion. The big crowd. I revelled in that."

The revelry was only just beginning for those of a Celtic persuasion. Paul Larkin recalls staying in the ground for an age and then dancing all along the Paisley streets and seeing Billy Connolly in a phonebox as he and his companions skipped along. The Celtic team, determined to make up for the lack of champagne consumed in the game's immediate aftermath, decamped back to the Grosvenor Hotel to celebrate their title win with what Murdo MacLeod remembers as "quite a party". "It was incredible just to be part of that day, to be part of that team. To win the title is always special. It was marvellous to be part of that whole run to the last day and to win the league like that, something that people still talk about now. There's always a wee twist and that's what keeps you going, but it's not often there's a twist as dramatic as that. That's what made it so special. If you win the league by 12 points with 6 games left no one wants to speak about it, win it on the last day like that and people will remember it forever."

All across Scotland Celtic fans were breaking into party mode, as Eddie Toner recalled. "The bus was bouncing all the way home. We were desperately hoping to run into Rangers fans as we passed Ibrox but they were long gone by then. We got back to the pub and the same landlord who'd told us we had no chance got us all a round. It was the only time he ever bought me a drink. I met up with my brother and dad and went down Gallowgate to celebrate with them in an Irish bar before ending up in town at a nightclub until the early hours. All my mates were out together. They knew I had won quite a few quid as well but obviously that didn't matter as much as us winning the league. It was just an amazing day. It was easily one of the best days I've had supporting Celtic and it's the same for anyone who was at Love Street that day."

The emotions felt by Hearts fans were the polar opposite of Celtic's, as Andrew-Henry Bowie noted when remembering the return of his older brother, Bobby, who had been allowed to attend the match. "He came home from Dundee and locked himself in his room for two whole days. All across Edinburgh and beyond there were rivers of tears, as one little moustached footballer destroyed our dreams to make himself an instant hero with Dundee, Celtic and even Hibernian fans. He broke my fucking heart. I try to imagine what my life would've been like if Hearts had won the league in 1986. It wouldn't have solved all my problems. But it would've meant everything, and I mean everything, to me. In 1986, it was the only thing I cared about. I was twelve years old when Albert Kidd crushed me."

Sunday, 4th May 1986

"I must confess it was an unhappy experience watching Hearts fail to clinch the Premier League title," wrote Doug Baillie for an edition of the *Sunday Post* that no Jambo wanted to read. "Everybody (barring Celtic of course) expected them to win it. So the scenes when the final whistle sounded were heart-rending. Grown men unashamedly cried. Fans in maroon sought comfort on the shoulders of their own wives! But what a tension-packed afternoon it was at Dens."

Baillie, a former Rangers player, was perhaps regretting that his colleague Ron Scott had not been left to cover the game taking place in his hometown that day but, as football fans awoke the morning after to try and make sense of the previous day's excitement, he was far from alone in wishing the outcome had been different.

"Other than your nearest rivals, most football supporters generally just see fans of other provincial clubs as punters they probably have a lot in common with," said Barry Davidson, who had watched the devastation unfold from the Dundee end. "You would chat to them on holiday and have a pint with them while speaking about football. So I think once the elation of winning two points and ending the season on a high subsided you realised what they had lost. Most neutrals would have loved to have seen them win it rather than either side of the Old Firm. We had our job to do but, in hindsight it would have been better if it had been done and dusted before Dens. This wasn't any normal hard luck story with a 'maybe next time' attached at the end. Safe to say this was a once in lifetime opportunity for them."

Reluctantly, Hearts fan Mike Smith agrees. "I'll likely never see Hearts win the league. That was our time and we lost it on the last day." When he woke up that Sunday, Smith was relieved to find out that his wife hadn't gone into labour while he wallowed in his own misery. His spirits, however, remained unlifted. "It's fair to say I wasn't feeling too good the next morning. I was numb. I was in shock that whole day. I was in shock for the next couple of weeks to be honest."

Fellow Jambo Bobby Mitchell was also suffering. "I mean, how do you get over that? The weird thing is, you feel worse for everyone else than you do for yourself. You think about the wee ones, how it must have felt for them. I'd made sure my sister's boys supported the Hearts. I felt guilty for inflicting this on them. Then the old boys who'd supported the team all their days. Then there was my brother-in-law in Australia. I'd imagined I'd be speaking to him on the Saturday night, both of us celebrating at other ends of the world. I didn't phone him and he didn't phone me. I knew he would know and couldn't face it. I only got a few hours sleep and I just kept lying there thinking about how bad I was feeling and how many other people must be feeling exactly the same or worse."

The day's media made painful reading, viewing and listening for those Hearts supporters able to face it, as every outlet wanted to focus on one of the most dramatic and historic occasions in Scottish sporting history. Recriminations were already beginning with regards to the comfortable nature of Celtic's victory. Former Parkhead strikers Frank McGarvey and Peter Mackie, and their teammates Tony Fitzpatrick, Billy Abercrombie and Brian Hamilton were among those to come under suspicion from those of a Hearts (and Rangers) persuasion who suspected supposedly 'Celtic-minded' St Mirren players of taking it easy on the day.

"I spotted a boy from my work and after shouting his name for about five minutes he eventually turned round and said 'Celtic are winning 4-0'. My heart almost stopped," was how Jambo Ian Proudfoot remembered half-time at Dens Park the day before. "Fucking Frank McGarvey, Tony Fitzpatrick and the rest of the 'Tims' at St Mirren were doing their job alright."

Fitzpatrick angrily denies the charges. "I felt absolutely terrible after the game. My team was St Mirren. I'd been at the club since I was 12 and actually chose to sign for them ahead of Celtic. The story has grown arms and legs over the years with people coming to believe Celtic had to beat us exactly 5-0 or something. It's nonsense. With Hearts getting beat 2-0 the same scoreline at Love Street would have won Celtic the league.

"My family were there watching and I had to look them in the face after. I couldn't have done that if I'd gone easy on Celtic. We all had families to support and in those days our bonuses were a big part of us getting a decent, living wage. Do you honestly think I would see my wife and kids go without rather than do everything I could to provide for them?

"Our goalkeeper, Jim Stewart, used to play at Ibrox and was Rangers mad. Our manager was an ex-Rangers player and there were other Rangers fans in the team. Were they letting Celtic win the league as well? Or were all of us, Celtic fans, Rangers fans, St Mirren fans and anyone else, trying our best for the team who paid our wages but it just didn't work for us that day? I wasn't conflicted in any way that game. The more high-profile your opponent the more you want to beat them. Look at some of the players Celtic had. Paul McStay, Danny McGrain, Mo Johnston, Brian McClair. They were phenomenal. They were pumped up to win the game and were totally on song. The goals they scored were incredible."

One particularly persistent rumour places McGarvey in the Celtic dressing room celebrating with his former teammates after the game. Fitzpatrick laughs at the story while Murdo MacLeod, who definitely was part of the Celtic celebrations, says there is "absolutely no truth" in it. McGarvey himself also addressed the rumour in his autobiography, *Totally Frank*.

"I have heard that I was in the Celtic dressing room afterwards drinking champagne. I didn't see any of the Celtic players after the game. And I have actually met Hearts fans who have said to me, 'That must have been some party you were at the night Celtic won the league in 1986'. I wasn't at any party. I was in the house with my wife and kids."

In his book, McGarvey admits that he had given less than his best against Celtic earlier that season. He had been controversially sold by the Parkhead club just weeks after scoring the winning goal in the 1985 Scottish Cup final and received a rousing reception when he returned to Celtic Park for the first time since rejoining St Mirren. McGarvey says hearing the fans sing his name sent him into turmoil and holds his hands up to not giving 100 per cent that day but is adamant nothing can be levelled against him for the title decider.

"There was a running joke that Frank McGarvey never used to try against Celtic," remembered Buddies fan David MacDonald. "I personally don't buy the conspiracy theories but if McGarvey never played well against them that day it certainly wasn't the only time. Celtic were magnificent that day and we were shite. It was a team with nothing to play for against a team with everything to play for. It's one of those things."

Billy Abercrombie, who played in midfield for St Mirren that day, called the claims "complete bollocks" in his autobiography, *Aber's Gonnae Get Ye*. "We got slaughtered in sections of the media, who were hinting that St. Mirren had 'laid down' to Celtic, in particular, ex-Celts Frank McGarvey and Peter Mackie," he wrote. "Admittedly, Mackie's miss of an open goal from four yards with the score at 0-0 doesn't look clever in the context of the argument, but this sort of miss was not uncommon from Peter.

"Despite Frank's views to the contrary, we were not a one-man team, so he cannot be accused of single-handedly throwing the game! What caused the problems for Frank was that he was seen congratulating his ex-colleagues after the full-time whistle. With hindsight, this wasn't such a clever thing to do, especially in front of the TV and press cameras, and it gave the ammunition to those aggrieved at what had happened. The suggestions that we 'laid down' were an insult to us as people, never mind our professional credibility."

Ron Scott, of the *Sunday Post*, backs the assertions of the St Mirren players. "Whether or not there were a few St Mirren players happy Celtic were champions that didn't mean they gave anything but their best that day," he said. "Celtic blew them away."

Mike Smith appreciates that it is sometimes easier to seek out a conspiracy to make sense of a failure but reckons his fellow Hearts fans who still believe McGarvey and co. opened the door for a Celtic title are pointing their fingers in the wrong direction. "I bear no grudges towards St Mirren or anyone who played that day. The bottom line is that even if I did believe they took it easy, which I don't, it wouldn't have mattered if we'd got the point we needed."

When the story of the 1985/86 is told, it is almost invariably done so in terms of Hearts losing the title on the last day in crushing circumstances after a long unbeaten run in which the underdog bravely took on more fancied foes. Less often is the focus on Celtic winning the league in a dramatic climax while playing the type of football that purists everywhere claim to prize above all else. Do that year's league winners get the credit they deserve?

"I think the stuff about the last day does the St Mirren players a disservice because there's no way they were giving anything other than their best," said Murdo MacLeod. "I was playing in that game and the tackles were flying in just like they always do. It doesn't bother me because we know the truth and we know we played brilliantly and won the league in some style. If you'd told me before the game they would be taking it easy I would have been happy! The reality is that they worked hard and had a flying start. Thankfully, they missed two or three early chances and once we survived those scares and scored ourselves then we got in control of the game. I felt at the time that we were on a good run and at no point did I think we were out of it. I was always confident. We kept going right to the end of the season and got the reward we deserved."

Eddie Toner also feels that Celtic's late-season form and resolve was exceptional but understands the focus on Hearts. "All we could do was to keep winning and put pressure on Hearts and that's what we did. It was a fantastic run of our own but compared to Hearts it saw us sneak under the radar a bit. It really was to the great credit of Davie Hay and the players. Look at that third goal in the St Mirren game, the amount of passes. The team had some weaknesses but it had top class players as well. The way we played that day, the iconic lime green strip, Danny McGrain playing while his career was winding down, the tension, the reaction when the goals were scored at Dens – it means so much to every Celtic supporter who was there.

"Hearts came out of nowhere. It was an incredible achievement, a great story so I do understand the papers and others concentrating on Hearts. They should've won the league. They got so close. There's something about that day that just sums up what football is all about. The anticipation, excitement, despair – it's what makes it so great."

For Eddie and his fellow Celtic supporters, Sunday offered plenty of options for continuing the celebrations. Many chose to head to Celtic Park, where some of their league-winning heroes were to take part in a pre-arranged open day that was turning into a procession.

"We were back in the pub on Sunday for 12.30 and kept on going," he recounted. "We never even made it as far as Celtic Park. It was a great afternoon to finish off what turned out to be a wonderful season for us."

One man for whom the season was still not over was Murdo MacLeod. Despite starring in the Love Street drama, and partaking in the celebrations at night, he was scheduled to play again the very next day. A testimonial match had been arranged for Kenny Dalglish to commemorate him becoming the first Scottish player to win 100 caps for his country and a team of home-based players, including MacLeod and managed by Alex Ferguson, were playing a side of Anglo-Scots bossed by Tommy Docherty.

"I never expected to be playing for Scotland at this stage or to see 100 caps and this could be my last time at Hampden," said Dalglish in the run-up to the game. "It will be a fairly emotional day, something special. Hampden has so many special memories for me."

The exiles side won 5-3 (with Dalglish scoring for both teams) though the result was of little consequence to the nearly 30,000 fans who turned out to pay homage to the man many regarded as Scotland's greatest ever player; one who the Tartan Army were hoping would become the first Briton to play in four World Cup finals that summer.

"It was strange to play the next day but it was magical for me as well," said MacLeod. "It was just a fantastic feeling to have won the league in such a manner and then to have the opportunity to play on Hampden in a game for a legend like Kenny Dalglish the next day just kept it going. It was incredible to be part of it all. I suppose it was strange to play two games in two days but it didn't affect me at all because I was on such a high."

The hero of the hour also had to cut short celebrations to play in his own testimonial. Dalglish, now player/manager of Liverpool, had wrapped up the league title for his side with the only goal of the game away at Chelsea the day before. The result put Liverpool beyond the reach of the chasing Everton and West Ham United, who were due to meet each other on the Monday in a match that 'King Kenny' had rendered meaningless.

Given the changes that football has undergone in the past 30 years, it would be unthinkable now for top clubs to release players for such an occasion at any time, let alone before all league fixtures were fulfilled south of the border. It would be equally unthinkable now for an international friendly to be held a few days before the season's end.

It is also hard to imagine in the post-Sky era that the climax of the English season would ever pass now as something almost incidental to events in Scotland. Scots had always taken a keen interest in the English game, not least because of the presence of a high number of their countrymen plying their trade at the very top level in England, but it was followed at a dispassionate distance via newspapers and television highlights. Many had an 'English team' but this was a soft spot that fell far short of the fanaticism they felt for the Scottish side they supported. Manchester United, Chelsea and Liverpool shirts were a rarity in Caledonian towns and cities.

It was another era but the joy that football fans experience in triumph and the despair they feel in adversity remain as acute as ever. As Celtic followers lurched from one party to the next, Hearts fans sought solace in solitude wherever possible. Any hopes that Alex MacDonald and Sandy Jardine had of keeping a low profile until they came to terms with their loss were quashed by another long-standing date in their diaries – the Scottish Football Writers' Player of the Year awards. MacDonald later said he thought his assistant would have to be dragged away from a darkened room at home to receive his award and Jardine admitted in *Score and More* that he would happily have given the ceremony a miss but for the fact "it was an honour for the club as well as myself and I felt that an example had to be set because come Monday morning Alex and I would have to lift the players in time for the Scottish Cup Final against Aberdeen."

MacDonald was also decorated at the event when he received a special 'Manager of the Year' award recognising the exceptional job he had done. According to MacDonald, neither member of the Tynecastle management team was much consoled by the recognition but they didn't have time to dwell on the events of the past 24 hours either. They had work to do. Redemption could yet be Hearts' if they could get over the disappointment of Dens Park and triumph over Alex Ferguson's Aberdeen. A difficult task at the best of times had been made many times harder by their last-gasp heartbreak. Their exceptional man management and motivational skills would be tested to the limit.

Saturday, 10th May 1986

Having won the Premier Division by seven clear points in each of the previous two seasons, Aberdeen's fourth-place finish in 1985/86 was, by their lofty standards, disappointing. The Dons' 44-point total was their lowest since Alex Ferguson's first season in charge seven years previously. It was also the first time for five years they went into the final day of the season without either already being champions or still having a mathematical chance of taking the title.

Aberdeen were effectively already out of the title race when the nation's armchair fans tuned in for their first taste of live Scottish league action on April 19th. The added strain of six European Cup games plus 12 domestic knock-out matches perhaps contributed to back-to-back home defeats at the hands of Celtic and Dundee United in the week running up to the Tynecastle clash that made the event something of an anti-climax to the TV executives who had identified it as a potential title decider. Had the Dons beaten the other two contenders they would have travelled to Edinburgh with the opportunity to reduce Hearts' lead to a single point. As it was they went in with the best wishes of Celtic, who had beaten Hibs 2-0 at the same time as United were being held to a 1-1 draw at Clydebank that proved fatal to their faltering title ambitions the day before.

Even the notoriously demanding Ferguson could find little to criticise in his players' efforts in 1985/86, however, as their league form was clearly the victim of their cup success. The League Cup was already in the bag, courtesy of the comprehensive defeat of Hibernian that had cheered the Hearts fans so. The Dons had also reached the quarter-final of the European Cup, where they came unstuck on their return to the scene of their greatest triumph as IFK Gothenburg progressed on away goals to a semi-final they were desperately unlucky to lose to Barcelona in a penalty shoot-out. Having ended the dreams of Montrose, Arbroath, Dundee and Hibernian on the road to Hampden, Aberdeen now stood on the brink of doing what no Scottish side other than Rangers and Celtic had ever achieved and winning both domestic cup competitions in the same season.

"We weren't challenging for the league after winning two in a row but I never took it for granted," said Dons fan Richard Gordon. "In seven years we'd won almost as much as we had in the 70-odd before that so it was obviously an unusual period in Aberdeen's history. You always wanted to win the league and at that time thought it was between us, Celtic and Dundee United and never considered Hearts as a possibility. There was an expectation and belief at the time that we would win a trophy or trophies and the players would have believed that too. Fergie's attitude was 'what did we do last season? Well, we must try to do better this year.'

"Every season we had the utmost confidence in the players and manager that we would win something so winning a treble or the European Cup wasn't an outlandish proposition. Any expectation of them had been settled down fairly early on but the prospect of winning two cups was definitely not a disappointment. I remember a whole sequence of draws in the league that left us struggling so by the time we started progressing in the Scottish it was clear we wouldn't be winning the league and the treble.

"I was confident of winning both cup competitions though, because our record in finals was so good by that stage but when you saw the run Hearts were on, you thought there would be a real battle ahead, especially if they went on to win the league. I wanted them to do it and didn't doubt for a second they would."

Deciding to give Aberdeen's last game of the season at Clydebank a miss, Gordon spent the final day in the company of BBC Radio Scotland's Alastair Alexander. "I was at home with the radio on and went through to the other room when I heard the shouts of excitement. I heard the name 'Kidd' and, like a lot of people, instantly thought it was Walter who'd scored. Then I realised the truth and listened to the to the drama unfolding. It was unbelievable. While I wanted Hearts to win the league as a football fan it was inevitable the nature of their loss would affect them and I was thinking how that would benefit us."

In a BBC preview of the upcoming game, Archie MacPherson noted that were the Hearts management team not made of stern stuff they would have been unable to withstand the emotional battering they had taken. Choosing to film the segment from the battlements of Edinburgh Castle, MacPherson reflected on the fact they were looking out "on a city that on Saturday night went into mourning for a cause that died so brutally."

"It's one of those sickly feelings that'll always be there," acknowledged MacDonald. "It'll never go away and it'll never get any better but that's the thing about football. It's an emotional game and certainly we were sick. The players are sick for the supporters. We're sick for the players and that's just the way it is in this game."

Jardine was equally as forthright while trying to put a gloss on the situation. "I've been in the game, for what, 22 years, and I would have to say that's the most disappointed I've ever felt but that's history now. That's behind us and we've got a Scottish Cup final to look forward to and I think the occasion will lift the players. Not everyone gets a second chance but we've got a second chance here with the cup final. So on the Monday morning when we got them in we sat them down and thanked them and congratulated them on their efforts and started trying to lift them."

Under normal circumstances, an upcoming cup final would occupy every waking moment for everyone involved with a club like Hearts. These were exceptional times, however, and MacDonald says management and players alike lacked the time and inclination to focus on the Aberdeen game while the league challenge was ongoing. It was only after the deep depression of Dens Park had set in that thoughts turned to Hampden. While the flu virus that had wreaked havoc had passed on, injuries and what the manager called a "collective wounded spirit" still had to be contended with.

As the film cut to a shot of Hearts fans queuing hundreds of yards down the street from the Tynecastle ticket office, MacPherson continued by observing that the previous week's disappointment "hadn't diminished the great appetite of the Hearts support for tickets. They'll go to Hampden on Saturday

30,000-strong. Hardly any of the younger generation remember the last time Hearts won the cup in 1956. They haven't celebrated since in quite the same way."

Continuing his cup final preview, MacPherson turned to Hearts' opponents and commented that "Aberdeen though have been the form team in finals in recent years, winning three out of the last four. Even in a transitional period they remain a formidable force and have to be clear favourites for Saturday."

"I think they must approach the game as favourites and with a lot of confidence," conceded Jardine. "I don't think there'll be the same pressure on us and we're looking forward to the occasion."

"As long as our players give it their best shot then we can't ask for anything else from them," added 'Doddie' almost sounding as if he was attempting to lower expectations. "They've done that since we started that run way back and if they can do that then I think it's going to be a good game."

The week following the Dens Park drama was proving eventful for the man who had brought to an end one of the most romantic stories in the annuls of Scottish football. In recognition of the service he provided to Celtic, Albert Kidd was a late invitee to a pro-am golf tournament held at Cathkin Braes the day after Dalglish's Hampden testimonial.

"Me and George McGeachie played. I was actually playing the guy Peter Thompson, the pro," he remembered. "I am on the first tee and it felt like there were a couple of thousand people watching us all tee off. Roy Aitken and Danny McGrain came running across. 'Oi Albert! Absolutely brilliant, wee man!' Andy Cameron was hosting it. He was a big Rangers man, of course, and he absolutely slaughtered me. He was like, 'What about that little bastard sitting down there'.

"I got about 25 letters sent to Dens, some with two pounds, some with three pounds. 'God bless you, wee man. Get yourself a pint'. I also got sent a piece of paper that a guy – a Hearts supporter – had wiped his backside on."

St Mirren's Frank McGarvey also received a similarly foul-smelling package in the days following Kidd's intervention but we will never know if they shared a pen pal or whether there were two Jambos hellbent on dishing out excremental retribution. Either way, the next piece of correspondence Kidd was sent was of a more sinister nature. "There was a photo of me with my young lads in the paper, and this was sent to me," he remembered. "It had the message 'Hope you feel smart about yourself, we are coming to get you' scrawled on it."

The scrawlings that Celtic fan Eddie Toner had to deal with were of an entirely different sort. His betting slips in many of the bookmakers of Glasgow's east end were ripe for collection. "I went into one of the bookies I had won from and the guy behind the counter was a Rangers fan. I had to pick up £240 and he told me they didn't have that amount of money and I'd have to come back later. I did and he still wasn't happy about giving it out. He said he only had it in fivers. 'I'm quite happy to take it in 2p pieces mate,' I told him. 'Ah, you were lucky,' he said, shaking his head. I took great pleasure in watching him count it out."

The odds that bookmakers such as Toner's acquaintance were offering on a Hearts victory in the SFA's showpiece final had been lengthening since 4.40pm the previous Saturday but, as the week wore on, Hearts players and fans began to mount something of a rally.

"I couldn't get myself up for the final," said Mike Smith. "I knew we wouldn't win and at the start of the week I wasn't going to Hampden. Aberdeen had a great team and after what happened we had no chance. Then Alex MacDonald, Sandy Jardine and the players were coming out in the papers saying how they were even more determined to win the cup now and I started to soften. On the morning of the match I said to my wife, 'Do you mind me going to the Aberdeen-Hearts game today?' She said she didn't. I never bothered telling her it was 140 miles away."

Sandy Clark says the only reason he managed not to cry in the aftermath of Albert Kidd's spectacular intervention was the consolation offered by the trip to Hampden. While convinced the team could put the setback behind them and triumph over Aberdeen in the cup final, the striker, writing in his autobiography, admitted some of his team mates were coping better than others.

"I felt fine going into the game although I think some of the younger players might have found it a little more difficult. I had never won the Scottish Cup and I was desperate to get my hands on it. We had shown over the course of the season we could beat the best."

On the day itself, kick off approached and Alex Ferguson and Alex MacDonald led their teams out to face 60,000 fans at Hampden to the accompaniment of a pipe band. Once the pre-match formalities were over, the Hearts players removed their tracksuits to reveal the silver away shirts they would once more be wearing. The Aberdeen team, who had signed off their league campaign with a 6-0 thrashing of Clydebank the week before, contained no less than six full Scottish internationalists and many of the greatest players in the club's history. For a team drained by a season of highs followed by a week of the most crushing low imaginable it was a daunting task but the Jambos were at least back to full strength. Craig Levein and Kenny Black were restored to the starting line-up having recovered from the bug that had laid them low while captain Walter Kidd, who had been a doubt during the week due to a burst blood vessel in his foot, had been passed fit to play.

Predictably, taunts about the previous week's events rang out from the Aberdeen end, while the Hearts fans responded by levelling allegations of bestiality at their rivals. As Clark had correctly identified, Ferguson and his charges knew the Tynecastle side would be vulnerable after their heartbreak at Dens Park and instantly took the game to their opponents rather than allowing them to grow into the match and forget their pain. The opener duly arrived after just five minutes, when John Hewitt cut across the Hearts defence to fire the ball low past Henry Smith from 18 yards. The Jambos had decent chances to equalise through John Robertson and Gary Mackay while Smith was forced to parry another Hewitt shot away to ensure there were no more goals in the first half.

"Aberdeen fans were making plenty of noise," recalled Richard Gordon. "Hampden was a second home to us. This was our fourth Scottish Cup Final in five years. Everyone was very confident, partly due to the fact we won finals and partly because what had happened to Hearts. That run lifted them onto a different plane but when you looked at the teams player-for-player, I wouldn't have swapped any of theirs for ours. Jardine and Levein were great but we had Miller and McLeish. John Colquhoun had a great season but we had Peter Weir. Frank McDougall had done great for us so I wouldn't even have taken John Robertson, who was their star. That's testament to what an incredible job 'Doddie' did at Hearts."

"I didn't wake up and think 'they might still win the cup', the day after Dens," said Hibee John Craig. "Quite the opposite really. I was convinced they would win the league and that would drive them on to win the double. They were only going to Dens to celebrate. Once the air of invincibility had gone you remembered that Aberdeen were probably still the best team in the country."

The second period began in almost identical fashion to the first, with a John Hewitt goal and though Hearts endeavoured to find a way back into the game, Neil Berry's effort cannoning off the bar was as close as they came to scoring. Substitute Billy Stark wrapped things up for the Dons with a header in the 74th minute and the Jambos' misery was complete when Walter Kidd picked up a second booking late on for throwing the ball at an Aberdeen player.

"I'd had a real dislike of Walter Kidd ever since he'd smashed Eric Black in a game at Pittodrie," said Gordon. "So him getting sent off while we were 3-0 up was the coup-de-grace."

"The frustrations came out," said Robertson on

TWTTTW. "The team by that time had gone. The legs had gone. The spirit had gone and we knew it was a season that ultimately we'd end up with nothing."

The last eight days had also caught up with Sandy Clark, whose dream of winning a Scottish Cup lay in tatters. "I felt bad after what happened at Dens Park but when the final whistle went at Hampden I felt far worse," he wrote. "It was almost like the feeling you have when you lose somebody close to you...we deserved to win something that season, we didn't and that was so hard to take."

Hearts fans were as broken as Clark and his team mates but that did not stop them once more staying behind to cheer the team who had come so near but yet so far and were now condemned to a season of second prizes. Despite missing out on silverware, MacDonald's side had the undying adulation of the 30,000-strong maroon army who stayed behind to show their appreciation and sang 'Championees' regardless. Perhaps conditioned by the events of the previous week, there was no repeat of the tearful scenes at Dens on the terraces as pride wrestled with pain for emotional dominance in Jambos' hearts.

"The final defeat wasn't nearly as bad as Dens for me," said Mike Smith. "We stood on the terraces at Hampden and celebrated what an achievement our season had been even though we didn't win anything. I felt a lot of pride that, at last, Hearts were back as one of the top teams in Scotland."

"It is almost incredible to think they've done so much and won nothing," said Archie in his commentary. "Well, won nothing for the record books but have won the respect of many people."

Perhaps there was even the glimmer of respect from those of a Hibernian persuasion among their relief and glee?

"While I have to admit to a little admiration for what they achieved in having such a long unbeaten run, I didn't admire their particular brand of football," said John Craig. "You can't help but sympathise and think how you would feel if it was you. You know how disappointed you are if you lose a game late on, imagine that was the whole season, the title, gone just like that. Despite them being our main rivals and enjoying what happened, I do sympathise with them. I can't help it. That said, as I watched Aberdeen brush Hearts aside I thought about how a season that had looked like being quite horrific had turned out to be quite pleasurable."

The bottom line, brutal as it may be, was that no matter how much Hearts deserved to win a trophy that season, they failed to do so. Regardless of how much neutrals got behind the cause of the underdog, it is hard to argue that Celtic and Aberdeen weren't worthy of their successes. The Dons had become the first non-Old Firm side to win both cup competitions in the same season. This remarkable achievement has been largely overlooked due to the focus of the 1985/86 season being on a side that failed at the final hurdle twice in eight days and forever have 'silver shirts, silver medals' jibes to endure from their Edinburgh rivals. Do the Dons, like Celtic, perhaps miss out on the accolades they deserve?

"I think Aberdeen and Celtic get the credit from their own sets of fans, who have wonderful memories of their achievements that season, but the abiding memory of 85/86 is absolutely the Hearts story," said Richard Gordon. "To be on the brink of achieving so much after proving everybody wrong and winning over so many people and yet eight days later you're a broken side with nothing. All those games without losing. It was absolutely crushing and I think every football fan can appreciate how they feel and that's why the story resonates to this day."

As the Aberdeen support began their journey up the road in joyous spirits, their maroon counterparts embarked upon the considerably shorter journey along the M8. For the second time in a week, cars, buses and trains were filled with football fans whose dreams had been crushed. For this to have happened once in a season was cruel, a second instalment of pain was bordering on brutal. Like the Celtic supporters cursing missed opportunities as they stood on the Love Street terraces with hope fast fading, it is impossible for Hearts fans not to look back throughout season 1985/86 and regret potential turning points – Paul McStay's stoppage time equaliser on the opening day of the season, the 6-2 defeat at St Mirren that impaired their goal difference, the Sunday kick off against Aberdeen that disrupted their routine or Bill Crombie's decision not to award a clear penalty at Dens Park. It is impossible to know what the butterfly effects of any of those incidents going the other way would be, but one inescapable fact is that with just minutes of the season remaining, Hearts' destiny lay in their own hands.

That for one side to win another has to lose is a sporting axiom and, irrespective of what happened at Love Street, Hearts lost the league title under their own steam in the most crushing fashion possible, an event of such devastation that it cast a dark shadow over their attempts to seek redemption at Hampden seven days later. Their efforts over the course of the season were heroic and led their fans to commit the cardinal sin of football supporters – they had allowed themselves to not just hope but believe. The footballing gods had given with one hand but, with expectations cranked up beyond fever pitch, they took back with the other at usurious rates of interest.

The pain of the double heartbreak was hardly helped by the fact the team were committed to attending a function at Edinburgh's Caledonian Hotel that everyone involved with the club hoped would be a celebration but would now be taking place in an altogether more subdued atmosphere. As the bus made its way along Princes Street, everyone on board was left stunned by what they saw. Thousands of Hearts supporters thronged the thoroughfare to welcome their heroes home. Having travelled the 31 games unbeaten and shared the same emotional rollercoaster, they were not going to let the trifling matter of losing the league and cup in such a wicked manner stop them thanking the players for everything they had done and showing their love for the club.

Alex MacDonald stepped from the bus and into the crowd, where he was instantly raised upon the shoulders of supporters and carried to the hotel. Sandy Jardine followed and was given the same treatment, as was every single member of staff who descended the steps of the coach.

"I don't think any of us could have foreseen the swell of support that would be outside the hotel," said Gary Mackay. "And I don't think any of us would be ashamed to say – I know myself – that emotionally we just lost it."

John Robertson was equally amazed. "Here were fans who'd had the heart ripped out of them. We'd lost the title in the last few minutes of the league. We'd lost the Scottish Cup final and yet here they were treating you like heroes."

The Hearts management team headed straight to their room, ostensibly for a beer before entering the function room, but also to let the tears they kept in check for the sake of the players run free.

Even 20 years after the event, MacDonald found himself unable to contain his emotions when discussing on *TWTTTW* the reception the side received. "That was serious stuff," said MacDonald. "That was greeting stuff again for me and Sandy up in the room. We couldn't believe it, with the supporters. It was absolutely fantastic." At that point this brave, proud man who had not only brought Hearts back from the brink but had once more turned them into a major force in Scottish football could take no more and asked for the recording to be stopped.

Saturday, 9th August 1986

It was a sign of the Old Firm's 1980s malaise that the 35,443 who turned up to see the league flag raised was the second-largest crowd Celtic had attracted for their opening home league match of the season that decade, Rangers being the visitors on the other occasion.

The fans clapped and sang as the championship trophy – won amid such drama and euphoria just three months earlier – was paraded but the biggest cheer of the day was reserved for one of their opponents.

With the presentation festivities and pre-match warm-up completed the teams made their way back to the dressing rooms but one of the away side's practice balls had to be retrieved from the far side of the pitch. Celtic Park's famous 'Jungle' erupted when its inhabitants saw who the responsibility fell to.

Dundee were the opponents that day and the emergency ball boy was Albert Kidd, whose elevation to full-on cult hero status with the Celtic faithful was complete.

An urban myth has Kidd taking a lap of honour around the track before the match, something the player stresses was not the case. "I remember that game versus Celtic vividly," he says. "It just worked out that I was last to leave after the warm-up and the ball went away over to the Jungle. I ran across to get it, hence the reason I was last by about 25 yards coming off the park. I will always remember the crowd standing cheering me. The hairs were standing up on the back of my neck.

"I never did a lap of honour but it was very obvious everyone was giving me an ovation and I applauded them back. Kenny Dalglish was at the game, and he spoke to me about the game at Dens, how good it had been for Celtic. I think there is a photo where Davie Provan has his hands up, gesturing 2-0 to me."

The match itself, Jocky Scott's first as Dundee manager following Archie Knox's summer resignation, didn't turn out well for Kidd, his team mates, or for the small Dark Blue contingent on the terraces. Maurice Johnston scored the only goal of the game but Celtic's superiority was evident in every department without them delivering a particularly polished performance. The new gaffer, considerably less taken with Kidd than the Celtic support, replaced him in the second half. Again the response from the home support was rapturous.

"As for the game itself, I remember breathing out my backside," said Kidd. "I was playing in a role wide on the left, where I needed to run up and down the park and it was not me."

It was not Celtic Park but another location where the events of 03/05/86 had been wildly celebrated that acted like a magnet for the nation's media that day, however. Having made his first appearance in the Ibrox dugout on the last day of the previous season, Graeme Souness was performing the other half of his player/manager duties for the first time. His Rangers team had travelled to Easter Road, where the home fans also sang the name of Albert Kidd, both in honour of his role in denying Hearts the championship and to wind up their opponents. It was a stormy affair on and off the park from the outset but a grenade was tossed onto Hibs' famously sloping surface in the 37th minute. Predictably Souness was at the heart of the action.

'The Battle of Easter Road' broke out when Souness lashed out following challenges from George McCluskey and Stuart Beedie, who had joined Hibs from Dundee United. McCluskey was left with a badly cut leg and lay in the centre of the park awaiting treatment as a 20-man brawl broke out around him, with only Hibs keeper Alan Rough staying out of the carnage. Once the match officials finally restored some semblance of order, Souness was rightly red-carded and several other antagonists were counting themselves lucky not to have joined him in being sent for an early bath. In all nine players were booked in a game that Hibs won 2-1.

"Although we were excited, we couldn't even be certain Souness would be a success," said Rangers supporter Hamish Strachan. "He had no managerial experience but we went to Easter Road hoping it would be what we believed it could be and the start of something special. And what happens? He gets sent off, we get beat and the bubble is burst!"

Regardless of the result, the Souness revolution had begun. Also making their debuts for Rangers that day were England internationals Terry Butcher and Chris Woods, the first of the high-profile signings from south of the border that Souness was to make. Rangers were able to offer European football at a time when clubs in England were banned after years of high profile hooliganism that had culminated in the 1985 tragedy at Heysel Stadium, where 39 fans lost their lives. UEFA had taken stringent action against the English clubs, excluding them indefinitely from competing on the continent. With funds to back his ambition, Souness persuaded a host of top English talents to try their luck in Glasgow during a stormy five-year reign that was to change Scottish football forever.

A huge Rangers support followed their team to Easter Road that day, sensing that their barren period was coming to an end but entirely ignorant of the seismic shift that their club and the wider game in this country was about to experience. Much of the narrative of the first half of the 1980s concerned fading empires – Rangers on their uppers and Celtic only just holding up to the challenge of young pretenders from the east. Reports of Rangers' death had been greatly exaggerated, however, and, to paraphrase one of the decade's most popular films, the empire was about to strike back.

"We got in Europe on the last day of the season and that was the objective that day," reflects Hamish Strachan. "Maybe we were disappointed Celtic won the league but the bigger picture, when you look back, is that Souness wouldn't have been able to bring in the players he did from down south if we weren't able to offer them European football.

"What impressed me was that he built the team from the back, which had been terrible the year before. Colin West was the first signing and people were scratching their heads wondering if this was going to be all we hoped it would then he brought in Chris Woods and Terry Butcher – a brilliant keeper and the England captain – and people were sitting back thinking 'this could be the start of something big'. It was the start of great times for us but back then we had no idea how special it would be. Gary Stevens, Ray Wilkins – these were big-name England internationals – came as well. We were in dreamland."

Hearts also had a chance to strike back on the opening day of the 1986/87 season when the fixture list afforded them the opportunity to avenge St Mirren for not giving Celtic a harder time on that crushing May afternoon. In the event, retribution was not forthcoming and the two sides played out a drab 0-0 draw, a result even more disappointing for the Edinburgh club given St Mirren were shorthanded for an hour following a first half red card.

It was not the ideal start to the season after a summer of torment for Hearts fans, although their ranks had been swollen with the arrival of Mike Smith's daughter a few months earlier. "A week after the Hampden defeat, my wife gave birth to our first child," he said. "Three successive Saturdays in May 1986 saw the three most emotional experiences of my life and, thankfully, ended with the joy and gift of a new life."

The baby's arrival perhaps balanced the departure of Jambo Bobby Mitchell for pastures new. "We had been planning on joining the wife's brother in Sydney for ages. We were actually planning to go earlier in the year but I put it off saying I had cold feet and wanted more time to think about it. In reality, I wanted to hold off and see Hearts win the league. My wife wasn't daft but she never forced the issue. She knew what it meant to me. I think some people still believe I emigrated because of what happened at Dens. That's not the case but it didn't make things more difficult, put it that way."

A further blow to the Jambos cause had come when *The Hearts Song* missed out on top spot in the charts to another poultry-related effort, Spitting Image's *The Chicken Song*, which, along with another 90 singles outsold the Tynecastle track during the week of its release.

Sandy Jardine had been elevated to joint manager but the arrangement was a short-lived one. Jardine left Tynecastle two years later, with chairman Wallace Mercer claiming the experiment with co-managers had failed to produce the desired results. But Jardine and MacDonald remained close friends until the former's untimely death in 2014 at the age of 65.

Alex MacDonald was sacked by Mercer in 1990 and became Airdrieonians manager, leading them to two Scottish Cup finals and into Europe during the most successful period in the club's history. He hasn't worked in football since leaving Airdrie in 1999 but was voted the 48th greatest Scottish manager of all time in a poll carried out by the *Herald* newspaper. He has also rightly been inducted into Hearts' Hall of Fame in recognition of his achievements. Had he succeeded in extending Hearts' unbeaten run to 33, or even 32, matches then he would undoubtedly have found himself dozens of places higher.

St Mirren manager Alex Miller was to become a regular adversary of Hearts when he replaced the sacked John Blackley as Hibernian manager in November 1986. Although Miller delivered the club's first silverware for almost two decades when Hibs won the 1991 League Cup (leading gleeful Hibees to sing 'No Cups in Gorgie' at every opportunity), his tenure was also marked by the club's worst prolonged derby record. He was in charge of the Easter Road side for every one of the 22 games Hearts went unbeaten against their rivals from 1989-1994 and managed just seven wins from the 40 competitive derbies that took place during his reign. However much Hibees celebrated Hearts' torment at Dens Park and Hampden, their own side certainly provided Jambos with much needed succour in the ensuing years.

Miller's appointment to the Easter Road hot seat was overshadowed by a far more significant managerial change that had taken place earlier the same month. For Alex Ferguson the lure of restoring Manchester United to former glories proved too strong to resist. Initially Ferguson failed to set Old Trafford alight but over the next 26 years he would win 38 trophies, including 13 Premier League titles and two Champions League titles. A CBE and knighthood followed as the Red Devils became one of the biggest global sporting organisations and Sir Alex became acknowledged as one of the greatest managers in the history of world football; a fairly impressive CV for someone once sacked by St Mirren.

Less successful was the World Cup campaign that Ferguson led in Mexico in the summer of 1986. Scotland had qualified for their fourth World Cup in a row and hopes were high that they would break through to the knock-out stages for the first time. As it transpired Scotland whimpered home after failing to register a win and with only one goal (scored by Gordon Strachan in a defeat to West Germany) and a single point against 10-man Uruguay to show for their efforts. The Scots undoubtedly endured more than their share of bad luck but there was severe disappointment that a better fight had not been fought. This was, after all, a squad talented enough that doubts over Liverpool captain Alan Hansen's commitment were enough to see one of the best defenders in the world omitted from the squad.

"You probably have to say that the Scots who played for Liverpool were the last world-class players Scotland produced," reflected Ron Scott. "Hansen wasn't picked for Mexico and Souness retired from international football after the World Cup. Dalglish missed Mexico through injury although he did play another couple of matches but that was the end of an era as well."

Despite their heroics throughout the season, no Hearts players managed to force their way onto a late flight to Central America, demonstrating once again how Alex MacDonald's side was greater than the sum of its parts, as well as the pool of talent the national team could draw on in those days. The 22-man squad that Ferguson selected starkly illustrates how Scottish football was utterly changed from the summer of 1986 onwards.

Scotland's pool for Mexico consisted of only three Old Firm players – Roy Aitken and Paul McStay of Celtic and Rangers' Davie Cooper. Souness was still listed as a Sampdoria player while Steve Archibald was plying his trade with Spanish giants Barcelona and no less than seven played for top-flight English clubs. Five Dundee United players meant they were the most represented club in the squad with four Dons and Hibee Alan Rough completing Scotland's World Cup complement. It is inconceivable that a Scottish squad could look even vaguely similar these days.

Ferguson's departure signalled the end of an era for

Aberdeen. As they paraded the Scottish Cup around Hampden on that sunny afternoon in May 1986, few would have believed that, after winning 10 trophies in less than a decade, the Dons would lift silverware only four times in the next 30 years.

"All the top football writers from England used to travel to Europe for Celtic, Aberdeen, Rangers and United matches because their clubs weren't in," continued Ron Scott. "Alex Ferguson was always very welcoming and accommodating to them. He wasn't stupid. He'd always fancied a crack at English football and knew having allies down there would help him. I've always suspected he saw the writing on the wall at Aberdeen as well. He'd already lost several of the Cup-Winners' Cup team and, while he was doing well to replace them, the new players were maybe just below the standard of their predecessors with more rebuilding to come. If you look at the Gothenburg game in 86, they went out on away goals to a decent team but, in all honesty, Aberdeen should have beaten them. The next season saw them knocked out by Sion of Switzerland who they'd hammered something like 9-1 on aggregate a few years before. I think he knew the time was right to move on."

Richard Gordon also believes that Ferguson realised he had achieved all he could at Pittodrie. "The disintegration of the Gothenburg team was already underway. Strachan, McMaster, McGhee and Rougvie were away and Eric Black was famously left out the cup final against Hearts because he'd agreed his move to Metz. Half the team were gone but we still had a very good side, obviously. There was no way of knowing what would happen next.

"I think everyone knew Fergie would move on to bigger things at one point but everyone expected him to stay to the end of the season. My first reaction was actually, 'well at least we'll still have Archie Knox' because that would at least give us continuity with someone who was well respected by everyone at the club."

As it happened, Gordon and his fellow Aberdeen fans were set for further disappointment as Knox, who had actually become Ferguson's co-manager after leaving Dundee, agreed to step back into the assistant role at Old Trafford. Ian Porterfield, a Scot who had played the majority of his career in England and had a patchy managerial record behind him, was given the unenviable task of following in Ferguson's legendary footsteps.

"It seemed a strange appointment," said Gordon. "We still had good players but it quickly became apparent that it wasn't going to be the same. How could it be? We eventually had a revival under Alex Smith but it would never be the same again. We were second three seasons in a row but only once really challenged for the league."

On that occasion, Aberdeen took their fight to the last day of the 1990/91 season only to lose 2-0 to Rangers on the final day, meaning Rangers were champions instead. The two clubs went into the match tied on points and goal difference but, with Aberdeen having scored the greater number of goals, all they had to do was avoid defeat.

"I felt exactly as Hearts fans had done five years earlier," Gordon adds. "I was actually working at the game, commentating for Northsound radio, and I felt absolute devastation. I kept my head down and did my job the best I could but it's probably lucky I was expected to do it from an Aberdeen point of view."

Few observers in 1986 would have guessed that Jim McLean had also won his final trophy as a manager. The New Firm's northern powerhouse was no more. The 1986/87 season culminated in Dundee United enduring Hearts-style despair as both the UEFA and Scottish Cup finals were lost in a four-day period, a turn of events enjoyed immensely by followers of Dundee. Once again, agony for one fan is karmic comeuppance to another and United's despair allowed Dundee fans, for whom Europe was to remain an elusive dream for almost 20 years, to forget their own shortcomings and revel in the despair of others.

United's conquerors at Hampden were St Mirren, whose supporters could reflect on the business begun by Alex Ferguson finally being finished, and the match remains the last Scottish Cup final where all players competing and both managers were Scottish. Rangers continued to plunder England for talent throughout the season and were crowned champions – for the first time since 1978 – with two games remaining. Their crowning took place at Pittodrie, symbolic given the power shift that Scottish football was experiencing. Souness, however, had only just begun to shake the foundations of Scottish football.

"I knew the Souness thing was massive right away," says Ron Scott. "I thought the only doubt was over his experience but when I heard Walter Smith was coming in with him then he had the experience and knowledge of the Scottish game at his side. It sent out a clear signal. They had spent money on a big name for the manager and were going to spend big on players as well. You knew it was the start of something big. Only he could have persuaded Maurice Johnston to renege on a promise to return to Celtic and join Rangers instead."

Contrary to the common misconception, Johnston was not the first Catholic to sign for Rangers. John Spencer was already on the club's books at the time, but Johnston's status in the game and the circumstances surrounding his capture ensured he was not just the most high-profile Catholic to join up at the resolutely Protestant Ibrox club but also the most controversial signing in the history of Scottish football.

Johnston was not just a £1.5million signing, a Catholic, a former Celtic hero, or a lifelong supporter of Rangers' bitter rivals. He was all those things, and he was putting pen to paper just weeks after posing in a Celtic scarf as it was announced he would soon be returning to Parkhead after two successful seasons in France with Nantes. This sensational news story spilled over from the back pages to the front and featured on the main bulletins of every major television network. Celtic fans labelled their former hero 'Judas', while a section of the Rangers support, for whom the unspoken rules about not knowingly signing Catholic players seemed a just and proper tradition, were equally outraged.

Allan Laing's article in the *Glasgow Herald* carried quotes from the general secretary of the Rangers Supporters' Association, David Miller, that amply demonstrate the climate into which Johnston was stepping. "I never thought in my wildest dreams that they would sign him," he said. "It is a sad day for Rangers. There will be a lot of people handing in their season tickets. I don't want to see a Roman Catholic at Ibrox."

In the end, next to no one at Rangers returned their season tickets or turned their backs on their club. Much of the outrage had been stage managed by the press in the first instance and few Gers fans were doing anything other than celebrating wildly when Johnston scored an injury time winner in an Old Firm derby just months after arriving at Ibrox. Whilst the Rangers-Celtic rivalry will struggle to clear entirely the cloud of sectarianism, giant strides made towards eradicating bigotry amongst the blue half of the divide can be traced back to a managerial reign that began on the same day as Albert Kidd was inadvertently becoming a cult hero amongst the other side.

Souness's ambitious recruitment policy continued to bear fruit and, aside from a memorable league-and-cup double by Celtic in their centenary year of 1988, Rangers were to utterly dominate Scottish football for the next decade. Top English talent continued to be attracted north – no fewer than six of England's 1986 World Cup squad would eventually come to turn out in Rangers colours – before the club turned its attention towards the continent and even further afield.

October 1986 saw the financial markets' 'Big Bang' moment when the London Stock Market was deregulated, but the Scottish football equivalent had already occurred. The game's direction of travel reflected the wider changes taking place across society. Old Firm domination meant that Scottish football had never been the most egalitarian of competitions but the late

1970s and early 1980s had shown how it was capable of throwing up the odd challenge to their hegemony. As was happening elsewhere, aggregate wealth was rising but so was debt as the gap between those at top and bottom grew ever wider and more clubs were consigned to relative poverty.

"I watched Rangers win their first title under Souness up at Pittodrie and watching them celebrate I wondered if it would ever be the same again," said Richard Gordon. "Two things changed Scottish football – the change of manager and the decision to spend money. That day you could sense how big it would be. He had the force of personality and drive that inspired people to follow him to Rangers. Previously Rangers had tried to sign Willie Miller but couldn't persuade him to leave Aberdeen. Suddenly there was a big imbalance that kept growing. It was the end of the era in which provincial teams could, under the guidance of an inspirational manager, take on the big boys at home and abroad, even though they lacked their financial clout."

It was not just Aberdeen, Dundee United, Hearts and others who were struggling to keep pace with developments at Ibrox. "Souness came in and they were spending crazy money," said Celtic fan Eddie Toner. "We just couldn't keep up and 89-95 was the worst period in the club's history. We only won three trophies that whole time and we were struggling badly until Fergus McCann came in."

"Fergus eventually came in and restored Celtic to being a giant club," agreed Richard Gordon. "Very quickly they were signing the calibre of players that only they and Rangers could afford."

If the events of 3rd May 1986 constitute a millennial moment it is because they mark the beginning of the triumph of wealth, the last time rank outsiders became romantic outriders for our own dreams. It is notable how few non-Scots played in the five Premier Division matches taking place that day, with Dundee's German midfielder Vince Mennie as exotic as any to take to the field, and how that changed in the intervening years. Very few of the foreign players to have graced Scottish football over the past 30 years were world class and a small minority were great. The majority were average while some were far poorer than the indigenous players whose places they were taking. Often they were overpaid and the overall consequences have not been healthy for either the national team or Scottish football in general.

The past three decades have in many ways been an era of fools gold characterised by a litany of dodgy financial deals, unfit and improper custodians, white elephant stadia and a reimagining of passionate fans as customers of secondary importance to the unedifying pursuit of diminishing returns offered by television deals. It was no longer about defence or attack or even victory and defeat. Everything was brand growth and market positioning, international finance and globalisation, a 'loadsamoney' transformation that mirrored the boom-and-bust inequities unleashed on society by Margaret Thatcher.

As Celtic and, particularly Rangers, overstretched themselves in an attempt to outdo each other and compete on the European stage, the more their domestic rivals, encouraged by irresponsible lending by banks, lived outwith their means in an attempt to 'keep up with the Joneses'. Since then almost one-third of Scotland's senior clubs have faced serious threats to their existence after mounting ill-advised and inherently flawed debt-fuelled spending sprees in an attempt to accumulate through speculation.

Of the top 10 clubs that May day, three – Hearts, Motherwell and Dundee – were placed in administration after racking up millions of pounds of losses, with the latter repeating the trick a second time for good measure. Clydebank have been lost to the senior game, while Rangers, the instigators of this avaricious epoch, fell far further than their pre-Souness struggles when they suffered the ultimate ignominy of liquidation in 2012.

"In the context of Scottish football, it is crazy to think that since Albert Kidd came on as sub the championship has never left Glasgow and that is unlikely to change anytime soon," reflected Dundee fan Barry Davidson. "Whatever happened to Rangers in the past few years, they and Celtic have got bigger since that day with Murray and McCann growing the Old Firm brand to something that is out of reach for any other club to compete with over nine months."

"We had no idea how utterly different Scottish football would become," says Rangers fan Hamish Strachan. "From then on it was us or Celtic who would win the league. The money changed everything, and when you look at what happened to us and other teams you wonder how it was allowed to happen. A lot of people have a lot to answer for."

"The game fundamentally changed after that day," said Ron Scott, who has continued to cover Scottish football over the intervening 30 years. If you look at all the events of that season and into the next – Jock

Stein dying, the Hearts challenge, Alex Ferguson leaving, Graeme Souness taking over at Rangers, Kenny Dalglish, the last Scottish superstar coming to the end of his career, the coming of live TV games – it was incredible. Scottish football was on the edge of revolution, there's no doubt about that."

Saturday, 21st December 2002

"Ladies and gentleman," cried the Celtic Park stadium announcer, "Please welcome the greatest player never to play for Celtic, Mr Albert Kidd!"

The reception Kidd received from the Jungle the season after helping Celtic win the league was both rapturous and understandable but this was a different level entirely. More than sixteen years had passed since that May afternoon and many in the crowd – some 20,000 more than were there to see the league flag raised in 1986 – were not even born then. Celtic were playing Kidd's former club, Dundee, and he had been invited to carry out the Paradise Windfall draw on the Parkhead turf at half time. Every man, woman and child in the stadium rose to their feet to acclaim one of the club's biggest cult heroes as he walked on to the park. The traveling support were also keen to show their appreciation for the man who had so nearly delivered the club's dream of return to European football, an ambition that would finally be realised with UEFA Cup qualification at the end of the season.

The visit had been organised by Paul Larkin, who had accompanied Kidd from their seats in the Celtic Park hospitality section. "It was amazing to stand in the tunnel and hear the noise get louder as he walked on the pitch. Alby did the presentation and all was good. When he walked off all you could hear were cries of 'God Bless you Albert!' A lot of his family were there that day."

Eddie Toner, watching from the stands, remembers the event well. "When his name was read out a huge cheer went up. Albert Kidd is a Celtic hero to anyone from that generation or even the younger fans who've grown up hearing the story. He became synonymous with that day at Love Street and there are even supporters' clubs named after him. People know his name more than some of our own players from that season."

"Two of my sons were there, as was my brother," recalls Kidd. "It is nice to be remembered, isn't it? Everyone has an ego but I am not that kind of person. I don't place a great deal of importance in it but it is nice as a Celtic supporter to get that kind of reception. I remember watching the Lisbon final at 10 years of age and admiring Billy McNeil, Tommy Gemmell, John Clark, Jinky, Willie Wallace, Bertie Auld, and Bobby Lennox. I got to know them very well over the years and that was flattering as they were true legends of the game."

The Dundee-Celtic match came when Kidd was visiting his family in Scotland for Christmas from Australia, which had been his home for the past 15 years and remains so to this day. He knew his time at Dundee was limited when Jocky Scott was chosen to succeed Archie Knox and the club freed him just before Christmas 1986.

"Dundee yesterday released forward Albert Kidd," reported Ian Paul at the end of an item about Dundee's city rivals that appeared in the *Glasgow Herald* on 16th December. "The 29-year-old Kidd is still the club's costliest signing…but manager Jocky Scott, who has recently bought Keith Wright from Raith

Rovers and Tommy Coyne from Dundee United, feels it 'is only fair' to give Kidd a free transfer."

"When Jocky got the job to be honest, my days were numbered," said Kidd. "He never rated me. That's what happens sometimes in football. He was desperate to get rid of me and quite rightly so – if it isn't working it isn't working. What was awkward for me is that his wife is very friendly with my wife. I remember he set up a deal for me to go to Kilmarnock, and I knocked him back – he wasn't happy.

"The only time I actually had a problem with Jocky was when I asked a favour of him. I had always been very, very keen on playing abroad and Davie Hay organised a trial with an American indoor soccer club in Kansas. The club was managed by Charlie Cooke. My request was that I go and have a look and if the contract was right for me I would sign. My kids were five and three and I needed some sort of security for them but the answer was a flat no. I just thought because there was a relationship there between our wives, he might have allowed me to go to America but he never. It was Graham Thomson, the Dundee director, who eventually called me into the club, and said, 'The manager wants to move you on, we will pay you X amount of money,' so I moved on. I was never ever going to be in Jocky's plans, and I never wanted to be, to be honest with you. We're fine with each other now."

After leaving Dundee, Kidd signed for Falkirk and helped them escape relegation in 1986/87. He then joined Morton that summer, but on the proviso that he would be released immediately if an overseas club came in for him. Kidd played three friendlies for Morton, including one against Arsenal, who he had spent summers with as a youth, before leaving for a new life 'Down Under'.

"I had offers to go back to the USA, from Cyprus, France and Austria," he says. "Then, at the 11th-hour, an Australian club came in for me. We chose Australia because of the lifestyle it offered. Good move as it turned out."

Kidd signed for West Adelaide, a Greek club in the South Australian city, and went on to enjoy success on and off the park, winning Player of the Year awards at both state and national competition levels and a pair of golden boots for being the league's top goalscorer. After retiring from the game, he moved into coaching as well as becoming a successful businessman. That day at Dens Park is never far away, however, and, as Kidd's reception at Parkhead so long after the event showed, his legend has grown over the years.

"I must say that, at the time, I really never appreci-ated how big a thing it was," he admits. "It was very clear some weeks and months later that it was a situ-ation that was an anomaly in Scottish football. It hit home how big a thing it was about a year and a half later, after I'd left.

"Some time later I met Billy Connolly at a hotel in Adelaide. I was coming out and he was coming up the main driveway. I waved to him and said how you doing, and he said, 'Ah, you're from Scotland'. Just then two girls come across for a photograph – want-ing it with Billy Connolly obviously. I said, 'all the best Billy, see you later' and he was like, 'Hang on, I want a wee chat with you'.

"They took the photographs, and he came across and asked what I was doing in Australia. I said I came

172

across here to play for a Greek club and he was like, 'Oh, you play football?' I told him I used to play for Dundee and that we were both Celtic men. I said 'I actually scored a couple of goals that helped Celtic win the league in 1986'. And I kid you not, he went, 'Fucking Albert Kidd!!!' He grabbed me on the steps, he was basically jumping around with me. He said, 'Pleasure to meet you'. I said the pleasure's all mine.

"He then said, 'What are you doing tonight? I have a show if you want to come. Come to the show and come backstage afterwards.' So I went backstage and was there for about an hour and a half. I ended up telling jokes to him! He was telling me he made £24 million off the banana feet video. I would guess this was four or five years after the Hearts game. I still had the moustache and feather cut happening. We've been in touch since.

"I played with a lot of really good players but I will be better known than nearly all of them. Every single year I get recognised. I have been in Venice, on cruise ships, in Mexico, everyplace I have been. A punter will recognise you or you say something, and the next minute there's another eight guys around you, saying, 'It's Albert Kidd!'"

Emigrating hasn't spared Albert the wrath of Hearts fans who still hold him responsible for costing them the league title. "Being in construction, I was on the sites a lot," he said. "There are a lot of Scots, especially in Perth, a lot of Brits. One guy on the site will go, 'Fucking hell, you will never guess who is working down there.' I have the suit on, they have the hard hats on. The next minute they are down giving me grief!"

One Jambo grateful not to have run into his nemesis in Australia is Bobby Mitchell. "We'd been living here over a year and had settled in really well when I got a call from a Hibee mate. 'Ha ha, guess who's going to Australia? Albert Kidd! You moved to get away from him and he's followed you.' I'm sure he's an alright guy who was just doing his job but I'm glad to be in Sydney and not Adelaide."

As it transpired, Kidd did have reason to visit Mitchell's new home city not long after he emigrated to Australia. "I got voted the Hibs player of the year by their Sydney branch and went along to collect the award to a brilliant ovation. I meet fans all over Australia all the time and I'm either loved or loathed."

Kidd's fame led to him pulling on the shirt of his beloved Celtic when he lined up alongside George Best for a charity match in Australia, while the affection with which he is held at the club has led to him becoming friendly with many of his childhood heroes. Irish/Celtic band Charlie and the Bhoys have written a song about him.

Hibees have come to venerate Kidd as much as Celtic supporters over the years and many refer to him as 'Sir Albert', with 'Albert Kidd Day' marked on various Hibs messageboards and forums each May 3rd. A photograph widely circulated on the internet shows the legendary Brazilian footballer Socrates holding an Albert Kidd t-shirt while Hibs fan and best-selling author Irvine Welsh used the events of that day at Dens as part of the backdrop for his novel, Crime. His name has also been given to at least one family pet.

"It was about six months afterwards that we got a

Jack Russell and I decided he was going to be called Albert," laughs Hibs supporter Colin Christie. "It was mainly to wind up Jambos but there was one day I was taking him for a walk in the park and there was this mental-looking Rottweiler running about. I didn't like the look of it so started calling Albert back. It turns out the Rottweiler belonged to this guy about twice the size of me with a maroon and white scarf on. He'd obviously heard me calling the name and was looking at me suspiciously. His dog could easily have eaten Albert and he looked like he could do the same to me so we made a quick exit before he started asking questions."

Is the man himself surprised about the impact he has had on people's lives and how his profile continues to grow thirty years on?

"It's crazy," Albert says, shaking his head. "I return to Dundee every year to see my family and there's a pub in Lochee called the Albert – but it gets called Kiddies. Bizarrely it used to be called Albert Kidd. There must have been another Albert Kidd at one point – I had my 18th in there. Anyway, even now when I go in, I don't put my hand in my pocket. I was in with my son one time and a punter came up and said, 'God bless you, wee man'. Steven asked if I knew him. I said I had never set eyes on him before but he will be a Celtic punter. Steven was like, 'That's unbelievable'. I was at a wedding last year and was in Kiddies beforehand. A couple of punters came up to me. 'Remember how you celebrated the second goal, can you do that again? I will take a picture. Please Albert. I'll buy you a double Scotch.' I had a kilt on. I wasn't doing that!"

"But it's been 30 years. And you start to think, what is it with people? There are more important things than football. It can get irritating at times but I have always been obliging. I am a decent bloke."

Celtic fans may not have been so welcoming had they known of Kidd's brief dalliance with 'the dark side'. "I kept in touch with Bomber," he said. "He is a good lad and called me up – 'I'm coming to Australia'. He was in charge of the Rangers youth team at the time, and it was a high-level competition - Juventus, Vasco da Gama, Newcastle, Liverpool, teams like that.

"Alan Hutton and people like that were in the Rangers team at the time. Bomber said, 'I want you to be my assistant. I was like, 'Fuck, I am going to have put a Rangers tracksuit on?' He said 'Ach, it's fine'. In actual fact I ended up living with them at the hotel. So I was the Rangers assistant at this huge event, and Rangers won it. People were coming across to the dugout and saying, 'Bomber, why have you got that Fenian bastard there with you?' I was putting on the accent and saying, 'but mate, I am Australian!'

"I remember I came back when Souness was at Rangers. Archie invited me to Ibrox. David Dodds was a good pal of mine, he was there. We went up to the lounge and had something to eat. Bomber came in, and he was very loud. Mark Hateley was there too. He came in and said, 'Fuck, it's that bastard who won Celtic the league, who let him in?'"

Kidd's name is invariably sung whenever Dundee meet the Tynecastle club but more to taunt the opposition rather than to celebrate their former player, who knows his chance to enter Dundee folklore passed three years before the Hearts game that changed his life.

"You know when United won the league at Dens I missed a header that would have stopped them winning the league," he says. "You can see it on Youtube, I remember it vividly. I just could not get above it. Had I scored there they wouldn't have won the league. It was the same situation. That would have been sweet.

"Football has changed so much since my day. In the 1980s there were lots of good teams and Dundee could beat Celtic or Rangers on any given day.

"After I left the game, I had a couple of opportunities to get back in, notably when 'Cowboy' McCormack was manager at Morton. He wanted me as his assistant. I've coached in Australia for years and with the business acumen I have, yeah I think I could coach in Scotland no problem. But life is good now and I wouldn't change it for anything. I have great kids and grandchildren. I feel fit. I still train but I like a bit of red wine and could lose a bit of weight. It's all good though. My life changed that day at Dens. I moved to Australia soon afterwards but it never left me."

It has never left Scottish football either, as Ron Scott acknowledges. "It was the most momentous end to a season ever. It had everything – drama, intrigue, joy, controversy and heartbreak – and there were so many teams still waiting to have their fates decided. The whole country was gripped by what was happening. When you look back now it's probably the most momentous year as well. It could be seen as the start of the modern age of Scottish football. We talk about 'Helicopter Sundays' now but that was a 'Helicopter

Saturday' without the helicopter, and Albert turned everything on its head with just seven minutes left."

The seismic changes the game underwent in the decades since did not happen because of Albert Kidd but a chain of events that can be traced back years saw him become the main protagonist in the most dramatic day in the history of Scottish football. Kidd achieved fame and infamy in equal measures for just seven minutes of a football career that lasted more than 15 years. As he freely admits, he became a household name while other, more talented footballers have been forgotten. He spent longer at Dundee than any other club but, aside from the dying minutes of the 1985/86 season, his time there was not particularly successful or happy, at least in the footballing sense. Had he not appealed for a last chance to impress, and had his teammate not injured his knee, Albert Kidd would have been a mere footnote in the history of Dundee Football Club, let alone in the history of Scottish football as a whole. Does Kidd believe there was an element of fate in the circumstances that contrived to change his life or does he see it as a coincidence?

"I have thought about this long and hard over the years," he says. "Big situations always seem to have a twist or turn. Two things are for sure, I was never in the plans for that day and I was surprised that Archie called on me to go on. Fate? Well, I guess maybe so."

Part of the reason why the Albert Kidd story continues to appeal is because it reminds us that the name inscribed on a trophy only ever tells part of a much wider and richer story. Those who make history aren't always the ones who win medals and caps.

Football has the capacity to throw up unlikely heroes who, in utterly unforeseeable fashion, change not only their own lives but those of countless others as well. No matter how much money pours in or out of the game, we can only hope that somewhere within the footballing fraternity there is space for the cult hero, the unfashionable and flawed, to make their mark.

He may have won the league for his boyhood heroes and become famous for far longer than his allotted 'Warholian' quarter-hour, but there is still the merest flicker of regret for Albert Kidd, Lord of Lochee and Leith, at the way his story is often told.

"What was disappointing about the whole thing, it was like I was not that good a player who got brought in at the last minute and was lucky enough to score two goals. It is frustrating in many ways to be considered a failure. If you speak to some of my teammates and ask them, 'What do you think of Albert?' they'll tell you I was a better player than I'm given credit for. But if things had worked out better at Dundee then I wouldn't have been on the bench that day and things wouldn't have turned out the way they did. Like I say, I wouldn't change what happened for anything. Although I do think I should have got a cap for those seven minutes!"

Saturday, 19th May 2012

Schadenfreude may be an entirely natural – if unattractive – component of our psychological make up, but for football fans it is also one with a particularly nasty sting in the tail. The more one hates his local rivals, the more he wishes misery upon them with every fibre of his being and the more joy he takes from seeing them fail, then the more he will hurt and the more embittered he will become when things do go right for them.

There were few Hibernian supporters left at Hampden by full time and the numbers remaining in the stadium by the time Hearts captain Marius Zaliukas climbed the steps to lift the Scottish Cup could be counted on one hand. His side had just thrashed their city rivals 5-1 in the first all-Edinburgh cup final for well over a century. It was the third time Hearts had won the Scottish Cup since their shattered heroes were swept aside by Aberdeen days after their devastation at Dens in May 1986. Hibs had last won it in 1902.

"You wouldn't wish it on your worst enemy," said Alex MacDonald of the heartbreak his side suffered in 1986, missing the fact Hearts' enemies across the city had been doing exactly that. "But that's football. That's why we love it and why we hate it" and it was not difficult to guess which side of Edinburgh was enjoying their ride on the game's emotional rollercoaster that May afternoon in 2012.

"Seeing Hearts lift the Scottish Cup in 1998, 2006

and 2012 exorcised some of the ghosts of 1986," said Jambo Mike Smith. "The 1998 win was actually my footballing highlight as it was redemption for Dens and came after we'd waited so long for a trophy, but a cup final is a cup final and to beat your main rivals 5-1 was special."

"It doesn't traumatise us like some Hearts fans think it does," claims Hibee John Craig. "Of course it was painful at the time, very painful. I never leave games early but I did that day. It wasn't so much about us being beaten, or even beaten by Hearts, it was because I knew what their fans would be like, goading us after the game. The way they go on about it though, it's a far bigger thing for Hearts than it is for us. I suppose some Hibs fans did keep mentioning beating them 7-0 though, so I can't blame them."

"We'd had our noses rubbed in the 7-0 game for 40 years," said Smith, "so 5-1 was revenge for that, for me. That was a meaningless league game though and this was a cup final, the biggest Edinburgh derby ever."

The cup final came little over a year before Hearts entered administration in an attempt to survive the £28million debt accrued during Lithuanian businessman Vladimir Romanov's controversial ownership of the club. Hibs fans were full of glee once more at the demise of their arch-rivals, who were hit with a 15-point penalty for going into administration and consigned to almost certain relegation the following season.

Hearts did indeed succumb to the drop despite a spirited battle mounted by the skeleton squad that the club's administrators left behind. But there was a sting in the tale for Hibs fans revelling in the Jambos' misery. The Easter Road club were presented with the opportunity to confirm Hearts' plight when they visited Tynecastle with little more than a month of the season remaining and Hibees arrived at the ground ready to celebrate. Not only did the 2-0 home win stave off relegation for the hosts but it also dragged Hibs further into the battle to avoid the drop themselves. They then managed to throw away a two-goal advantage from the first-leg of a relegation play-off with Hamilton Academical and were demoted from the top tier on penalties in front of their own fans. Both Edinburgh clubs spent the next season in the newly rechristened Championship and were expected to fight it out for the runners-up spot behind Rangers who, three years after their liquidation, were looking to make it back to the top flight.

As it transpired, a reborn and shrewdly run Hearts side romped to the title and the automatic promotion spot. Hibs and Rangers both fell at the play-off stage, condemning them to at least another season in the second-tier. The Leith side had somehow contrived to turn what should have been the springboard to a lengthy period of unquestioned city dominance into a nightmare from which they, much to the delight of Hearts supporters everywhere, have yet to escape.

"Both my daughters' partners are Hibs supporters," admits Smith. "The Christmas we were in administration and headed down I got a present from my daughter's fiance. It was a road map and I thought, 'what do I need a road map for?' Then I looked inside and he'd circled Dumbarton and Cowdenbeath and all these places we'd be going to in the First Division. I thought it was pretty funny, to be honest, but I was laughing more when they chucked away their two goal lead in the play-off and managed to get relegated as well. That was Hibs' Albert Kidd moment for me."

"The Albert stuff is fairly tongue in cheek," said John Craig. "Certainly for me it is. I'm happy to banter back and forth but I'm never comfortable with the really poisonous stuff some fans come out with. At the end of the day it's just someone who happens to support another team. I suppose it doesn't make sense when you think about it."

Deriving pleasure from the misfortune of rivals is a key component of the psyche of most football fans. It may even be the dominant emotion of the diehard. Very few clubs outwith a small elite ever achieve real, tangible and sustained success. In that context, the travails of others provide sustenance through lean times, relative glory that takes on extra significance in an environment where the emotional investment in the fortunes of your side is so high.

Emerging victorious from a fiercely contested derby a couple of times a season or finishing higher in the league allows supporters to look down their noses at their foes, deny their own obvious failings and say "well, at least we're not as shite as them". It means victories in minor battles can be celebrated even as a much larger war is being lost. However much they deny it, football people derive their identity and sense of self-worth in no small part through their standing relative to their enemies. The pleasure they feel at a rival's tribulations becomes almost as intense as the joy they experience at those rare moments of triumph for their own side.

The back-and-forth between followers of the two

capital clubs mirrors rivalries around the world. Each version has its own history, myth and legends. The enmity may vary in its intensity and its local dynamics but the essential ingredients remain the same – two sides that intensely dislike each other for largely irrational reasons. The events of May 1986 remain hardwired into the rivalry between two of Scotland's finest clubs as well as continuing to be the subject of wider controversy.

The publication of Sandy Clark's autobiography in 2012 re-lit the fire under the affair, particularly when he claimed "I am friends with one of the players who played for St Mirren that day…I know he gave it his all but he has admitted to me that some of his teammates hadn't been so professional. Some of them were happy to see Celtic win the league."

The allegation once more drew furious rebuttals from several players who played for St Mirren that day, including Frank McGarvey, who told the *Paisley Daily Express*, "Sandy Clark ought to be ashamed of himself…We were on a big bonus to win, so there was a lot at stake for us too. We went out that day and played the best we could…Hearts had it in their own hands that day. They bottled it – plain and simple."

Tony Fitzpatrick was equally angered by Clark's accusation, saying, "It was very disappointing what Sandy said because I'd always seen him as a warrior and had so much respect for him as a top player and top man. I would never accuse him of not trying against Rangers because he supports them and I wouldn't do it to any other professional either."

Clark also criticised the decision to appoint Bill Crombie, who turned down his penalty claim early in the game, as that day's referee. "I believe the football authorities made an absolute mess of things by appointing Bill to our game," he wrote. "Everyone knew Bill was a Hearts fan, it put enormous pressure on him...The last thing he would have wanted was to be accused of favouritism towards Hearts but in that penalty call he went too far the other way."

The man in the middle that day was certainly far from immune from its fallout, with Mike Smith saying, "I interviewed Mr Crombie for a job several years later. He didn't get it." But Clark's public dissatisfaction brought former Dundee player John Brown into the fray to defend the referee. Never one to shy away from controversy, 'Bomber' told the *Daily Record*, "If Sandy wants to point the finger at anyone then maybe he should look at himself as he dived. It was a blatant attempt to win a penalty and I remember telling him at the time that he was a diving b*****d."

Brown went on to accuse the Hearts players of bottling the big occasion, with Craig Levein, in particular, coming in for withering criticism for calling off before the game. He was later to clarify his remarks in a typically forthright manner in another newspaper interview. "I'd have said to Craig that day: 'You've never won a medal in your life and you only need a draw to become champions – if you're shittin' your pants, big deal.'"

All St Mirren players who have discussed the matter have continued to deny the charge that they took things easy on Celtic that day. Whether there is any truth in Clark's assertion or not, short of his acquaintance going on the record to criticise his former teammates or a deathbed confession from a member of the St Mirren team, it will remain conjecture. Allegations that Levein "shat it" will also remain part of the legend that has grown up around Saturday, 3rd May 1986. As with all legends, people will choose to believe the parts they like and discard others.

"If we'd won it, we wouldn't have half the column inches or half the amount of people talking about it," said John Colquhoun on *TWTTTW* as he acknowledged that Hearts' falling at the final hurdle had actually given rise to a better story. "Or half the amount of interviews or half the amount of media space that we've had because of what happened. And I would trade it all, everything, to just get a goal with ten minutes to go at Dens Park. No question. Because we deserved it."

Halley's Comet was visible from earth for the first time in 76 years on February 19th, 1986. It was the same day that the Jambos stretched their unbeaten run to 23 matches – leading contemporary wags to note that the comet came round more often than Hearts' title challenges. Their epic run would see the Edinburgh side exceed all expectations and win hearts and minds across the country and beyond, before the dream fell apart right at the end.

The comet is scheduled to pass us by again in 2061. Perhaps the fairy tale will spawn a sequel with a happier ending before then.

Acknowledgements

An enormous amount of thanks are due to a lot of people who helped me put this book together in record time. With apologies to anyone I have left out, they are: Albert Kidd, Ron Scott, Richard Gordon, David Farrell, Frank Marra, Alan Pattullo, Ryan Law, Paul Larkin, Eddie Toner, Mike Smith, Bobby Mitchell, Chris Rich, Michael Grant, John McGarry, John Craig, Colin Christie, Tommy Young, Fraser Kirkwood, Barry Davidson, Tony Hamilton, Joanna Chisholm, Alan Cheghall, Andrew MacLean, David McLeish, Murdo MacLeod, Tony Fitzpatrick, David MacDonald, Alan Wilson, Hamish Strachan, Chris Collins, Iain Munn and Dave Martin. Peace and love to you all, whoever you support.

For their unstinting support and love I thank my family, particularly my wonderful wife, Vicki, and my beautiful son, Elliot.

Clubbed to Death
Grant Hill

*A fantastic example of Scottish contemporary writing.
Funny as f****
Hardeep Singh Kohli

A very funny, no-holds-barred romp. Really rich stuff.
Neil Forsyth

Packed with gags from start to finish.
comedy.co.uk

Two Men. One Dream. No Clue.

When Andy Brennan's father suddenly dies of a lifelong Scottish diet, his grieving son decides it's time to make his mark on the world and create his own musical utopia.

So he and his brother-in-law Cornelius, an eternal opponent of common sense, buy a nightclub. But not just any nightclub. One with a highly suspect safety record. That keeps shutting down and re-opening under a new name. And during the worst economic downturn since the 1930s.

But Cornelius has somehow discovered the world's greatest undiscovered disc spinner – the soon-to-be-famous DJ Quantum – and identified that structural investment, refurbishment etc all play second fiddle to buying the world's biggest mirrorball.

Welcome to Club Quantum, where mind-melting music expands horizons like a demented cross between the Hacienda and Haight-Ashbury. But sandwiched between the bus station and the homeless shelter.